The Interactive Marketplace

The Interactive Marketplace

KEITH BROWN

McGraw-Hill

New York   San Francisco   Washington, D.C.   Auckland   Bogotá
Caracas   Lisbon   London   Madrid   Mexico City   Milan
Montreal   New Delhi   San Juan   Singapore
Sydney   Tokyo   Toronto

Library of Congress Cataloging-in-Publication Data

Brown, Keith (Keith T.)
    The interactive marketplace / Keith Brown.
       p. cm.
    ISBN 0-07-136343-2
      1. Electronic commerce. I. Title.

    HF5548.32 .B76 2000
    658.8'4—dc21   00-041577

McGraw-Hill

A Division of The McGraw-Hill Companies

1 2 3 4 5 6 7 8 9 0 AGM/AGM 0 9 8 7 6 5 4 3 2 1 0

ISBN 0-07-136343-2

Printed and bound by Quebecor World/Martinsburg.

McGraw-Hill books are available at special quantity discounts to use as premiums and sales promotions, or for use in corporate training programs. For more information, please write to the Director of Special Sales, McGraw-Hill, Two Penn Plaza, New York, NY 10121-2298. Or contact your local bookstore.

This publication is designed to provide accurate and authoritative information in regard to the subject matter covered. It is sold with the understanding that neither the author nor the publisher is engaged in rendering legal, accounting, or other professional service. If legal advice or other expert assistance is required, the services of a competent professional person should be sought.
—*From a Declaration of Principles jointly adopted by a Committee of the American Bar Association and a Committee of Publishers.*

To my cherished best friend and wife, Rebecca;

To my buddy and son, Ian;

To those at BuildNet who are making my dream into a reality;

And to my savior Jesus Christ, who has given me
the insights contained herein.

Contents

Acknowledgments   ix

Introduction   1

1   The Rise of Interactivity   15

2   Being Controlled   37

3   One-to-One Marketing, One-to-One Service   67

4   Mass Customization: All Products One of a Kind   103

5   Everything Is a Commodity; Nothing Is a Commodity   131

6   Delivering the Whole Product   157

7   The Death of Competition as We Know It   189

8   The Vortex Effect   211

9   Community Is the End Game   231

Index   237

Acknowledgments

The ideas and concepts in this book, I believe, can have far-reaching and consequential implications for the way business is conducted around the world. But like any worthwhile ideas, they did not come to me all at once, nor were they created in a vacuum. Indeed, the influences on me over time were just as far-reaching and consequential, starting with the devoted support and love of my parents, Brevard and Doris; and my brothers Phillip, a computer wizard, and Vance, an attorney with business acumen and the ability to sell. Phillip and Vance both helped me put code and feet to my ideas in the launching of BuildSoft and BuildNet. At BuildNet, I owe a long salute to the folks who have stuck with the company as it has grown from a single good idea to a billion-dollar company that employs over 1000 people. These people include my friend since the second grade Bill Waddell, who played a key role in all the details; Jeff Andre, who was there when I first challenged our company with the daunting task of rolling out an e-commerce company, long before e-commerce was fashionable; John Price, who never stopped selling the ideas even in the early days when no one would listen; Bob Weston, Dan Rich, David Barkhau, Rusty Ray, and Barry Tutor, who all took care of delivering the message to the home-building community; Lamar Phillips, Boyd Poisel, Jeff Oliver, David Buffaloe, Tanya Seeley, and Jean Racz, who kept many different parts of the company running; Mike Bright who always made us look great; and Steve Thompson who made us all feel secure. Here I have named only the first people who came into this organization and are still here today. There are many others, now about 1000, and each individually has contributed to making my dreams a reality. For all of the builders in this great BuildNet family, now building over 43 percent of all homes in the nation, thank you for believing in our shared dream to make construction a *pleasurable experience*, accomplished with quality, speed, and affordability. And I want to especially thank my editor and agent, John D. Wagner, for his belief in this project, his indefatigable support, and his wise editorial counsel.

Finally, I would like to thank all the hard-working folks at McGraw-Hill, especially my editor, Michelle Reed, who early on saw the potential real-world impact contained within the ideas in this book. Michelle backed this project and argued for it from the moment she first read the manuscript, and her support has made all the difference.

Keith T. Brown

Introduction

Astute watchers of the Internet economy have recently recognized two distinctly different business models in place today. One model, which is typically launched from browser-based (Web-based) information infrastructures, invents a technology and through its value-added service offerings expects to draw a community to it. This model is flawed in at least two ways (and lately Wall Street has been increasingly skeptical of this approach, with stock valuations sinking accordingly). First, if one company can purchase a Web-based technology, and dress it up with logos and customized interfaces, others can too. Amazon.com has learned this lesson the hard way. Amazon.com was an early adopter of browser-based order and fulfillment services, and it got a jump on market share with a truly original idea. But Amazon.com has seen its market share eroded as the technology its service depends on is proliferated by competitors in every one of Amazon.com's vertical markets, no matter how fast Amazon.com adds verticals to its product offerings, be they electronics, tools, videos, music CDs, auctions, etc. This technology proliferation cheapens the originality and luster of Amazon's once-original style of taking and fulfilling consumers' orders, and it dilutes Amazon's service offerings. Look at the inverse, asymmetric rise of Amazon.com's marketing expenses to its income, and you will see that they are frantically struggling to keep people returning to their site. As Web-based retailing becomes increasingly common, the only thing Amazon.com has to differentiate itself from the strikingly similar

1

product and service offerings of its competition is *marketing dollars*. Since it can't really deliver original technology or vastly superior service, it has to lure potential customers to its site much as vendors of other historically undifferentiated commodities have lured their customers: with bells and whistles; smoke and mirrors.

More importantly, though browser-based services have introduced new interactive communication tools to the economy, they have not revolutionized the creation of products they offer. Instead, the Web allows interaction with HTML pages, but essentially links the information to old-fashioned back-office systems that "rip and read" the information, just as they did before the Web existed. At the fulfillment end of the exchange, the vendors grab information off the Web, often by printing it on a purchase order or packing slip, and act on it by packing and shipping a stock product. This is an old-fashioned business-to-consumer ("B2C") model that essentially converts a paper-based information exchange to a computer screen. Yet this is hardly an improvement over the way business was done 100 years ago. Instead of writing a product request on paper and mailing it, you e-mail it in through a Web page. If it weren't for the Web interface, you could easily sit in a stock room at the fulfillment end of this exchange and execute the same order fulfillment you would have done in a nearly identical stockroom in 1900. Sure, the Web-based approach makes doing business easier and smarter, but at the end of the day, it is a technological challenge to take information entered in an HTML environment by a consumer and structure it so that it can move across supply chain enterprise resource planning (ERP) systems—the systems that manage inventory control, accounting, work orders, and purchase orders—and allow that information to intervene in the custom creation of the products that consumers themselves have designed. *That's* the wave of the future. *Not* static Web pages. *Not* rip-and-read models.

Optimally, this information exchange between the supply chain, the manufacturer, and the consumer would allow the consumer to manipulate an image of what they want to buy, and data would spin off that image, requiring very little or no human intervention to integrate it into the actual production of the product in question. But this can't be done simply with the Web. With Web-based presentations of information, each person interacting with that information would have to stop, see, read, process, and interact, on a case-by-case or order-by-order basis. In the end, Web-based systems are only slight improvements over old paper-based models, and—much more crucial to the theme of this book—allow customers to do nothing more than use an advanced electronic media to choose from stock products in a warehouse. Plus, as mentioned above, even if you purchase the latest Web-based technology, others can too. So, there needs to be a higher digital life form if the economy is to move beyond static document servers enabling the delivery of stock products. That, in the end, is not a very big step over the way things were done before the arrival of the Internet.

THE RISE OF BUSINESS-TO-BUSINESS MODELS

Unlike browser-based services, business-to-business ("B2B") models of economic exchange have not only gained widely positive recognition lately, but they are also the darlings of Wall Street. Why? Two reasons. First, a solid B2B model can bring substantial efficiencies to the ordering, manufacture, and delivery of products, while fulfilling the promise of easy customer interaction that consumers have become accustomed to in Web-based systems.

What is B2B?

In the simplest terms, a B2B system is a data translation or data mapping protocol that lets different computer platforms talk to one another in very smart ways. For instance, when you withdraw funds from an ATM that doesn't belong to your bank, you have engaged in a B2B transaction. If you have an account at First Union, and you use an ATM at a Chase bank, the ATM from Chase speaks with the master computer of First Union. This B2B transaction is made possible because the banks got together and data mapped their computer systems so they could talk to one another, even though they may have been on different systems or platforms. When you withdraw $40 from an out-of-town ATM, a universal code is generated by that transaction so that any bank that needs to know that $40 was withdrawn is instantly notified, in its own native language and computer code; a "business to business" transaction was completed.

Moreover, B2B systems work best when they allow information to be shared across integrated systems. An *integrated system*, in its simplest form, is a checkbook program like Quicken®. When you enter information once, the computer program distributes that information to other data fields in the program, without demanding that you repeatedly reenter that data. Integration is smart data sharing, where the data automatically populate the data fields anywhere in the system. Your $40 withdrawal needs to show up in your checking account register, the bank's master debit records, your branch office records, and the records of the bank where you got the actual cash. Yet you didn't have to enter it in each computer, nor did anyone at the bank. The data was integrated across these systems wherever the data field demanded the record of that $40 withdrawal.

To continue the ATM example, B2B systems can get rather sophisticated, as you will see when we touch on this same example later in the book. Let's say you withdraw money from an ATM in France or Mexico City. You receive money in the local currency. So the B2B exchange between that foreign bank and your bank is not just a simple automated debit and credit, but a cross-language, cross-currency protocol that had to check currency exchange rates in real time and make a detailed calculation.

Early B2B successes, like cross-platform international-bank fund transfers or the simple convenience of being able to use one ATM card at a foreign bank, were monumental accomplishments when they debuted, as they automated the exchange of information across computer platforms and information protocols. Using these successes as models, we now see the proliferation of highly successful B2B models in today's marketplace in many industries. We will visit other examples later in the book, but Wal-Mart's supply chain management solution is an excellent example of a B2B success. When you purchase a product at Wal-Mart, simply scanning that product at the cash register alerts the Wal-Mart supply chain to the absence of that product from the shelves. The information is shared, in a seamless integrated fashion, to all the stations in the supply chain that need to know that this product has been purchased. That information populates the back-office ERP systems that run the inventory, shipping, and accounting for the product suppliers, as well as the master and local back-office systems at Wal-Mart. These systems are loaded with an expert knowledge, and they "know" that when a fourth can of oil, or the sixth tennis racket, or the twelfth bottle of shampoo is sold off the shelves at the Wal-Mart in Williston, Vermont, it is time to ship more. There are no phone calls to make to order products; no paper-based purchase orders; no human intervention is needed to process the information required to replenish those shelves. The supply chain *flexes* in response to real time to that demand data. The data flow through data maps, so that any platform linked to Wal-Mart's can read and act on that data automatically. These efficiencies have saved consumers millions, and made the Walton family one of the richest in the world.

But take note: Systems like these, even when working optimally, deliver stock products. They have not yet figured out a way to allow consumers to intervene in the creation of what they buy.

THE NEXT STEP: INTERACTIVE B2B2C MODELS

It's now clear that business-to-consumer (B2C) product delivery systems, whether enabled by Web sites or in more traditional settings like brick-and-mortar stores, will gain efficiency by using the Internet. But even working at peak performance, traditional B2C systems will reach maximum efficiency and peak profitability only when integrally linked to solid B2B backbones. In other words, going back to that ATM example, it would not make much sense for banks to allow cross-bank ATM use, if each bank had to manually do the debits and credits on paper for each withdrawal, and physically shuttle those papers to the bank where the money would ultimately be withdrawn. In that case, you would have a sophisticated user interface (the ATM), but a back-office system still using business practices from the 1800s. So too with Web pages. If a customer uses a Web page to communicate with a company, it is an inefficient way of doing business to have that

Web page linked to back-office systems run by 200-year-old practices. You need a B2B backbone in place to process the information gathered at the consumer interface and communicate it seamlessly across integrated platforms in a way that allows it to populate the data fields required to do business smoothly and efficiently.

It is becoming clear that even working B2B2C models that integrate information across platforms are flawed. Why? When they are optimized, working at peak performance, they are set up to deliver *stock products*. Even though a system may have the most advanced integrated platforms in place, and data maps drawn to enable universal connectivity, many current B2B2C models will not reach their true potential because all they can do is deliver stock products. They do not allow consumers to interact with the design, creation, or manufacture of the products they will consume. And that is the crucial element required to bring optimum success to any forward-looking business plan that positions itself to take optimum advantage of today's technologies. A B2B2C model will reach peak profitability only when the platforms and business systems it links together can reach all the way down to the consumer and allow them to intervene in the design and creation of the products they will consume. Without allowing customers to design the products they will consume (or to choose from a variety of stock products to put together in custom systems or assemblages), the most sophisticated B2B platforms have limited value.

How can consumers actually intervene in the creation of the products they buy? That's where today's cutting-edge technology comes into play. Today's successful B2B2C model must be able to reach from the manufacturer, through the supply chain, through the contractor and point of sale, and deliver interactive capability to the consumer in an extremely friendly technology interface. The B2B2C system design must incorporate not only cross-platform automated data transfer capability (remember the ATM example), but two other crucial features as well:

1. The B2B2C system must have consumer-facing technology that allows consumers to use virtual tools to design the product they will consume, and this technology must allow supply-chain-wide seamless links so that the product design specifications created by the consumer can be shared across computer platforms, all the way up to the point of production or assembly. These product design specifications will likely be generated by a configuration management tool at the consumer end; one that employs a computer-assisted design (CAD) tool that lets the consumer manipulate an image of the product they want to buy, adjusting it to their custom specifications. But it is imperative that this data be formatted so it can be shared in an integrated format with the product production machinery, so the specification data spun off of the manipulated image can be incorporated directly into the machinery that will build or assemble the product.

2. The B2B2C system must also have systemwide cross-platform transparency, so that "demand-side" data (product specifications generated by the consumer) can be captured and shared with any link in the supply chain. This allows those on the "supply side" to gain valuable foreknowledge of consumers' demands which helps them balance inventory, delivery resources, and— for the manufacturer—even raw material purchases based not on what consumers might buy (stock), but on what they have already paid for or have expressed a specific desire for (custom). That's why the consumer marketplaces of the immediate future, indeed the marketplaces springing up around us right now, are *interactive marketplaces*. The technology lodged in these interactive systems enables consumers to intervene in the production of what they will consume, allowing the one-to-one delivery of custom products that are created at mass-production speeds and costs.

The logical extension of this is a world with no stock products, no inventory; it is a world where the supply chain is fully optimized to allow a product to move from manufacturer to consumer in such a way that the product briefly touches each link in the supply chain, as it moves toward the consumer. Moreover, this is a world quantum leaps ahead of the Web-based business models floated out there today, where consumers use static Web pages to choose from among stock products.

Another principal difference between the browser-based B2C models (Amazon.com, Buy.com, Ebay.com, E-loan.com) and integrated cross-platform B2B2C models—whether they have configuration-management tools embedded in them yet or not—is that the browser-based model hopes to *lure a community to its site* hoping that they will use an increasingly common technology. Unfortunately, "switching costs" among systems like these are extremely low; it's as easy as clicking a mouse to see whether Amazon.com, BarnesandNoble.com, or Buy.com has the cheapest copy of the latest best-selling book. But in the B2B2C environments the successful enterprise engages existing communities; delivers them sophisticated software tools; data maps among the platforms of the business entities that serve their needs; and enables easy commerce and seamless data exchange. This approach entwines the communities of users in the B2B2C platform, raising switching costs as a natural byproduct of delivering highly valuable services and custom products direct. For an example, imagine the naturally high switching costs to a consumer (what some call *stickiness*) if the customer had to choose between configuring a custom computer using easy-to-use online software, where that custom computer is delivered direct for less than the cost of a stock product *or* fighting traffic to shop among stock products at stores that de facto add into the cost of *your* computer the fractional carrying costs and overhead required to keep *all* their computers on the shelves. The switching costs from store to store are very low, because the consumer has no allegiance, no service incentive, and no cost incentive to stay faithful. But with the configuration-managed, just-in-time custom delivery system (similar to Dell computer model today), consumers will return again and again to this vendor. Additionally, because companies like Dell carry no inventory or stock (and very little parts inventory, if the enterprise is managed correctly, as it is at Dell), and no retail infrastructure costs, the consumer gets a custom product for less cost than stock. The switching costs are naturally very high, driven not by entrapment of the customer, but by value-added service companies like Dell that can deliver with frightening consistency.

Savings found with true B2B2C business models are found not only in optimizing the supply chain, but in reducing inventory, carrying costs, and by allowing data to be used to precisely predict consumer demands on a one-to-one basis. Indeed, this approach can even allow allied vendors to predict the needs of customers they have never interacted with before.

Clearly one of the keys to a successful B2B2C interactive marketplace model is to have easy-to-use, easy-to-integrate configuration-management tools that the consumer can use either to select and assemble products or actually draw them to their liking. (This is categorically different than the "click and buy" Web site approach, where consumers choose from among stock products using essentially static presentations of information.) In the

B2B2C model, information contained within the configuration tool can be sent to the pertinent player in the supply chain, *without* engaging the consumer in the engineering details of that product's creation. If, for example, the consumer "drags and drops" a furniture fabric into place on their custom couch, the work orders and purchase orders required to execute those specifications, order the materials, arrange their delivery, and even pay for the products, can all be background functions that precipitate out of the simple dragging and dropping of the fabric selection. This is possible only because the B2C configuration management tool is "hard wired" to the B2B delivery system, which has been designed to allow integrated, automated cross-platform sharing of data.

Without this kind of seamless information sharing, the consumer would work in one medium—a consumer-based electronic software product, or even simple sketches on paper—that must be "dumbed down" (printed) and reentered into the suppliers' design and procurement systems, and then dumbed down again to switch platforms to the manufacturer. The costs associated with this are widely acknowledged to be between 4 and 8 percent for each link in the supply chain. And that's just the information processing costs. Add to this the costs saved by optimizing the supply chain through reduced inventory, reduced finance carrying costs, reduced insurance exposure, reduced returns, reduced shipping and reshipping costs once the products are in the field... and you come away with the substantial savings industry analysts have been confidently floating out there: 35 percent cost savings across the supply chain on products delivered using B2B2C systems. One chief executive of a leading window manufacturer interviewed during research for this book claims that his company can save 20 percent off their bottom line by getting the custom window specification data from the field from those who want custom windows. That manufacturer has a production system in place to produce custom windows as fast as the system used to produce stock windows. Indeed, that production system is ready to integrally incorporate field specifications. Linked directly to this, the manufacturer has contracted with a delivery system that can deliver the custom window to any site in the United States just nine days after it is ordered. So, the B2B structure is in place. The reason the window maker isn't delivering custom windows on a full-time basis is that they lack the data. They lack the specifications from the field. The system breaks down at the "...2C" link of the B2B2C system. Even when the window manufacturer gets the data, it has to be reentered into the window makers' window production system. Once the "...2C" link is enabled, and the B2B2C links have cross-platform data-sharing capability, this window maker will be able to put out custom windows 20 percent cheaper than stock—and that's just *his* costs—to say nothing of the additional savings that come from reduced information processing costs and zero-inventory savings once the system takes full advantage of the B2B backbone.

In summary, today's economy is poised for dramatic efficiency gains by adopting B2B2C systems linked to configuration management tools that allow consumers to make the modern economy a truly interactive marketplace. In the late 1990s and early 2000, we have seen economic growth averaging around 3 percent or more per year, year in and year out, and yet inflation has stayed largely in the background. That is partially because of the efficiency and productivity gains realized by computer systems sharing information, allowing more production of goods, while concurrently allowing the containment of the most inflationary aspect of the economy: labor costs. Information processing labor has been reduced across many industries, as has redundancy of effort. But even more waste can be squeezed out of the system. The 35 percent savings that are the promise of a truly interactive marketplace that delivers just-in-time custom products offers an even more dramatic advancement in worker productivity and continued, low-inflation growth. Indeed, for low-margin industries (companies working on net profit margins of between 1 and 8 percent), it's completely within the range of possibility to see a doubling of profit and earnings ratios, without a doubling of infrastructure growth or an increase in gross expense. All because of the efficient interactive, cross-platform management of information.

Intrigued? Join me in future chapters to investigate the possibilities of business plans based on interactive B2B2C models.

1

C H A P T E R

The Rise of Interactivity

EXECUTIVE SUMMARY

The Internet-enabled world of e-business is at last perfecting economic exchange, which until now has stumbled and bumbled along in an effort to please customers. First, ancient economies all over the world perfected low-volume, consumer-focused custom production; then modern economies perfected low-cost, high-volume mass production with no consumer control. Until now, no one has combined the two to perfect low-cost, customer-controlled mass customization. But now the tools of the Information Revolution are finally enabling just such a thing. How? By directly linking (through computers that can talk across platforms) the customer's time-sensitive needs integrally to the means of production and by formatting this information in such a way that products and services can be mass customized, individualized, and delivered just-in-time on a one-to-one basis. But unlike past transactions, computer-enabled or not, that may have been similar to this, the information gathered to enable this mass customization is not discarded once the transaction is complete. Instead it is shared (with the consumer's permission) among complementary alliances of product and service vendors in a way that allows them to refine, on an individualized basis, the customization of a wide range of products and even to predict customers' precise future needs. Curiously, the result of this is a reversal of traditional economic exchange, as it shifts from static isolated exchanges where customer profiles and customer input were not utilized, to dynamic interactive exchanges where the customer is the primary source for product configuration information. That information is retained, categorized, and integrated back into the system to prepare it to better deliver future products and services. Whether a consumer is shopping for books, prescription drugs, or airline tickets, today's Web sites—when properly integrated to a sophisticated enterprise resource planning (ERP) system—are increasingly capable of remembering your billing records, shipping addresses, and buying patterns, and, based on your profiles or even what community you live or work in, suggest other products you may want to purchase. Plainly, the shift in control that accompanies this type of interactive economic exchange is nothing short of revolutionary. Control that used to be in the hands of the producer (who dictated product and service types to captive consumer markets) has now shifted into the consumers' hands, as they are now demanding products and services created individually, just for them.

With mass production shifting to mass customization, and control shifting from the producer to the customer, we are seeing an equally historic reevaluation of trusted maxims, some of which we have inherited without question from as far back as the Industrial Revolution, 250 years ago. Indeed, computer power and interactive e-business—the sale or purchase of goods and services through seamless (often automated) communication of the consumers' need-based specifications dispersed in an integrated format throughout the supply chain—*has given us a renewed sense of historical perspective. It has finally allowed us to reach back through history and pick only the very best aspects of all past models of economic exchange, and integrate them into an interactively linked economy supercharged with the tools of the Information Revolution. American Airlines recently researched, by zip code, the dates for school vacations in target communities across the country, and after sorting that list against their frequent flier club members, e-mailed reduced fare offers to parents, available just when they'd have time off. The sell-through rate was remarkable, and the e-tickets were arranged over the Internet. So, instead of offering trips through mass marketing, there was a highly targeted, one-to-one offering of products, across computer platforms, with the e-tickets credited and fare charges debited all seamlessly, in a highly efficient and profitable way. This ticket offering is simply combining the highly personalized one-to-one care we used to get from local travel agents who knew the school schedule, with the airlines' sophisticated computers that can arrange these trips as a mass customized offering. The offering combined the best of all past economic eras. See Figure 1–1.*

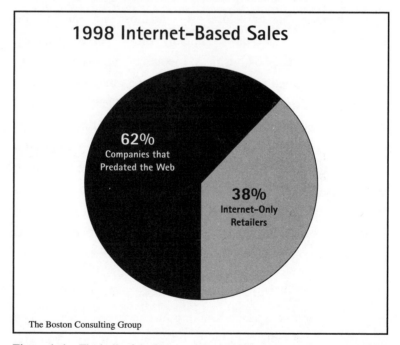

Figure 1–1   The bulk of the Internet sales in 1998 did not come from Internet-only retailers like Amazon.com and CDNow.com. It came from businesses that were in existence before the Web.

A trip to the mailbox can tell you a lot about how we are struggling to shake off past influences of mass production *and* how we are in dire need of adopting a more interactive future. Open your mailbox these days, and what do you see? It's *not* personal letters (those now come by e-mail). Instead it's catalogs, mass mailings, junk. Mostly, there are "shotgun" style appeals. Someone wants you to buy something. And these folks are just pouring these faceless, cold appeals out into the economy by the millions. Why? Amazingly, it's in the hopes that just a tiny fraction of the target consumers—perhaps 3 percent—will buy something. The tragedy, of course, is that the vast majority of these appeals just end up in the recycling bin. Why? They aren't truly targeted. The companies that send these mailings know no more about me or you than our addresses—and those they bought from another catalog or mail order company for $80 per 1000 names. If I ran a computer parts business, I would be almost as likely to get catalogs related to my business as ones that sold holiday candles, tins of nuts, or accessories for my car. That's because all that these mass mailing companies know is that I have bought *something* from someone in the past or that I have requested a catalog in the past. Indeed, sometimes it doesn't even take that much to earn a place on a mailing list. All you need is a phone number and address and you'll receive a direct-mail sales pitch. Your address ended up there because your local phone book was scanned by a computer and the addresses within turned into mailing labels.

When appeals aren't coming in by mail, they're pouring in by phone, with telemarketers calling just as you're sitting down to dinner. These calls come with little respect to who you are, your economic status, or your past buying patterns. You're being called just because you have a phone. And when mail and phone have exhausted you, there are TV ads and billboards along the highway. But advertising presentations don't even stop at the roadsides. I call it "ad creep," as ads are starting to show up literally everywhere you rest your eyes. There are ads on the backs of shopping carts, on bags, on people's hats, shirts, and shoes. Marketers are even putting ad stickers on fruit, so even when you're selecting apples or pears at the supermarket, you're getting an appeal for the latest movie or TV show. Appeals made to get you to subscribe to a magazine subscription are a classic example of the ineffectual nature of this shotgun appeal. If you are a new subscriber to a magazine, it likely cost that magazine more than $30 to get you to send in a check... not a great return on investment for a $12.95 subscription. The magazine has to induce you to renew at least twice to recover its money and get into the black. Besides being an annoying intrusion, this approach to sales is extremely costly and inefficient. It wastes our time, pollutes our entertainment environment, private time, and home lives with messages we'd just rather not hear, taxes our waste disposal system, and puts pressure on our forests and the environment. (A recent story on the news reported that a man was actually heating his house with junk mail, by getting *on* as many lists as possible!) But most of us don't like shotgun appeals. So, why does it continue? Because it is still the cheapest way to reach people who might, *might*, be interested in a vendor's product or service. Huge numbers of people are splashed with ads in the hopes that a tiny fraction of them will respond. Vast fortunes are spent on spokesperson's endorsement contracts, film production, and ratings or circulation research, all so that a 30- or 60-second ad, a billboard, or a magazine ad might motivate a few interested people to go into a showroom, make a call to a sales department, or hand over a credit card number.

Worse, this wasteful behavior of shotgun appeals doesn't stop with advertising. It spills over into the stores. To ensure that you will have enough choice when you finally decide to go shopping, when the ads finally get you into the stores, the stockpile of products is massive, all managed on a "just-in-case" basis. Stores routinely keep more goods on hand than they can possibly hope to sell. (They do eventually sell these goods, often at a discount, but efficiency is measured in turnover per year, when it can be measured over a much shorter length of time.) Why do we need such large inventories? Since retailers can't exactly target what consumers are looking for, nor have a product waiting that has been made just for you, they have to carry a vast assortment of many products to ensure they have the one product on hand that you find suitable. Cumulative carrying costs for the production, shipping, storage, and insurance for these goods are simply passed along to you, the consumer, no matter what you buy. That's because all these carrying costs, overstock, and reduplication of effort just drive up operating costs, and that must be reflected in the costs of the products the stores *do* sell.

Wouldn't it be a more efficient system if vendors had a better idea of who their potential customers were? Wouldn't it be a better arrangement, with far less wasted time, money, and resources, if vendors had profiles of potential customers, and could produce just enough products to fulfill *real, known* needs?

Let's take that even a step further, because this is the promise of a computer-based Interactive Marketplace, a.k.a. *e-business*. Wouldn't it be an ideal economic situation, indeed what *all* of economic history has aimed to accomplish, if the vendor not only had a clear idea of an individual customer's specific needs, but could customize a product specifically for that customer, on a one-to-one basis, no matter how many customers existed? That would be the crowning achievement of all economic history.

Or would it?

The next step would be if the vendor not only knew the customer's existing needs and was able to customize products to fill those needs, but also used the accumulated information about a client to actually *predict* the client's future needs and deliver the products "just in time," with customized service as a standard feature. But as you think of this scenario—something that's coming true right now, by the way—imagine the information necessary to power this kind of economy. The information must flow seamlessly from computer to computer, across platforms, within universal information templates or across data maps that allow all involved in the creation, manufacture, delivery, and sale of a product to automatically accept and integrate pertinent information into their systems, as they tie it integrally to the very means of production, delivery, and sale.

Is this a possible future? Computers talking to one another, allowing consumers to specify their products, often through automated calendar-driven systems? Yes. It's the promise of e-business; the promise of universal transactional systems linking the stations on the supply chain with the consumer *before the product is even produced or shipped*; the promise of consumers being able to communicate their individual wishes and, by doing so, dramatically reduce the waste and inefficiency which eats up so many dollars in today's market.

No more shotgun ads, no more junk mail piling up in your mailbox in the hopes you'll buy something. No more TV ads broadcast out to billions in the hopes a few thousand will buy. All vendors can now have a one-to-one relationship with each and every customer. Now that's a future we can all aspire to and be proud of when it arrives. Is it coming? Is it even possible? Read on.

A WALK THROUGH TIME

When we look at the potential future of economic activity, we don't have to invent much to come up with a perfect scenario for the exchange of goods, services, and money. We can simply take the best aspects of economic exchange throughout time, borrowing the best parts of the various economic ages throughout history. For the interactive marketplace, let's take a look at what we are borrowing and from where.

You don't need a Ph.D. in economic history to see that the world of exchange of goods and services can be roughly broken into two periods, the precapitalist society and the capitalist society. The capitalist society can then be broken down into the different periods that we all read about in our high school history classes: preindustrial society, industrial society, postindustrial society, and the information age, which rose concurrently with the age of the service industry. We are, of course, riding the crest of the wave of the information age and are just about to plunge headlong into a revolution within a revolution: the age of the interactive marketplace.

In the precapitalist society, power and wealth were concentrated in royal or lineage-based hierarchies of power. No matter how hard anyone worked, his surplus labor value (what today we call *profit*) was always in service of the king or ruler. Consequently, there was little or no opportunity for individuals to build wealth. Workers were not in control of the means of production. And what happened to the money they rendered to the king? Part of the community's profit was used to glorify the king with stately castles and high living. But part of it was also used to muster armies. A minimally successful community could afford a standing army of defense, while a truly successful community could afford an imperial army that could conquer others, and take advantage of even more subjugated peoples' ability to create, but not retain, wealth.

What was the means of economic exchange among the average citizens, the people who had little or no money? It was often barter, where products and services were exchanged for other products and services, in small-scale arrangements involving limited numbers of people who often knew one another. But more interesting, and more pertinent to this discussion about the interactive marketplace driven by computer technology, let's take a look at *how* services were rendered. Services were rendered one-to-one. They were customized, always on an individual basis. When you went to a cobbler, he knew your shoe size and the idiosyncrasies of your feet, and he could assemble custom-made shoes just for you. The same for the tailor, hat maker, house builder, mason, and blacksmith. These tradespeople and craftspeople were working with such a small community of people, it was easy for them to remember what exactly their clients wanted. This arrangement had its limitations, surely. In fact, it worked only because it operated on such a small scale. If you were to put it to the test, and ask for the mass production of goods and services, say, by requesting that the cobbler create 1000 pairs of custom shoes, the system would have fallen apart. The cobbler didn't have enough control over the means of production to produce 1000 different shoe patterns. And he didn't have a record-keeping system efficient enough to keep track of that many records. But for those customers that the tradespeople or craftspeople did service, there was nearly complete satisfaction, the best products of their day. Even better, since the community was so small, the tradespeople and craftspeople could easily see the condition of their products as they were used. They could see when a thatch roof was falling down, when shoes wore out, a wall crumbled, or a horse needed shoes. As they saw their products in use, tracking their service lives, they could *predict* what services their customers required, when they were needed, and deliver them just in time. They could come to the consumer and offer those customized goods and services, perhaps before the customers even realized their own needs.

Political upheaval, based largely on workers' inability to accumulate wealth and control the means of production, brought about the changes that would lead to the Industrial Revolution, which most historians agree ran for around 100 years, starting in 1750. It's important to cite the date and duration of the Industrial Revolution to show how, in so short a time, a "disruptive" technology—in this case, specialized tools and the invention of machines capable of mass production—could cause such massive changes in the world economy. (Analogously, look at computers and the Information Revolution, which have caused *even more* upheaval in a third of the time, and promise to bring changes of untold magnitude over the coming years.)

The Industrial Revolution brought forth a foundation-shaking transition from small-scale, stable agricultural and local commercial communities, which had their roots in Medieval times, to full-blown modern industrialism. The imperial and colonial voyagers of the European powers during the fifteenth and sixteenth centuries had opened the way to worldwide commerce, and these industrialized nations, mostly in Europe, intended to grow rich producing and selling their goods and services at home and abroad. The reason they could safely engage such large economies is that they had machines that could churn out a nearly limitless supply of products. We see the arrival of spectacular inventions like Watt's steam engine, Arkwright's spinning frame, and Cartwright's power loom. These machines not only gave workers control over the means of production, but they allowed engineers to study their operation, improve their efficiencies, and by analogy take mass production as a science to other areas of production, like agriculture, building, printing, and the management of information.

Unfortunately, the Industrial Revolution and the invention of machines capable of mass production came at a price. The industrial economies strayed from the small-scale, village-based economies of the previous millennia, and the so-called modern industrial economy lost its ability to provide personalized goods and services. What replaced it? An economy based on machines that could create a seemingly limitless supply of goods, with a one-size-fits-all approach. Sure, there was dramatic change: The owners and controllers of these machines—and even some workers—finally had control over the means of production and were able to create and retain personal wealth. But the price the communities paid was a terrible one, with dramatic implications for the economies of the future. Is *terrible* too strong a word? No, because the wasteful remnants of the Industrial Revolution are still evident in your mailbox when you sort through the junk mail: massive numbers of easily produced products, all the same, created under the rash assumption that lots of people will want to buy exactly what everyone else is buying, without any attention to personal service or the differentiated needs of the customer.

The Industrial Revolution did teach us something valuable. Though we lost the personal service and one-to-one exchange of customized goods from the pre-Industrial Revolution, we gained the ability to make machines that could produce products on a large scale—and these machines and technologies would improve over the years, to a high degree of refinement, allowing everyone a higher standard of living.

If we were to go back in time and choose what economic benefit we could take from each of these two economic periods, the answer would be obvious. The ideal contemporary economy would somehow combine the personalized services and customized products of the Medieval age with the mass production of the Industrial Revolution. Unfortunately, it is just as easy to pick out what was wrong with these two economic periods. In fact, it was obvious back then, especially in the Industrial Revolution. By the time of London's Great Exhibition of 1851, which was meant to celebrate the Industrial Revolution, many leading philosophers of the day were already expressing their distaste for industrialism: A worldwide economy dependent on mass-produced material goods; poisonous byproducts; dehumanized workers; and shoddy, poorly designed, mass-produced products. At this time there was even a backlash against the Industrial Revolution. Artists and craftspeople sought to return to a Medieval artists' "guild style" of making goods and services on a small scale. But that largely faded out around the turn of the century because the efficiencies of machines was too great, and the sheer number and variety of inexpensive, mass-produced products simply overwhelmed the custom craftsperson, whose products were inevitably far more expensive. Consumers were willing to live with less expensive products that weren't exactly right in exchange for the cheaper price. As for custom products, only the rich could afford them.

The Industrial Revolution still exerts a powerful influence over today's economy. Look at how efficient mass production is. In fact, it is so efficient, we don't even need skilled workers to run the machines anymore. Jobs can be exported to countries that have unskilled workers who will work for so much less that products can be made on the other side of the world, shipped to market, and still be sold at a healthy profit. Skilled American workers who used to operate those machines have now focused on creating service-based economies within the Information Revolution, where the "products" sold and the companies valued are based not on things you can hold, but services and products of the imagination which can save you time, money, and work. Prime examples of these are products like expert system software that allows people with no engineering background the ability to design viable structures; computer systems in whose hard drives are lodged the accumulated knowledge of generations of sales expertise; demographic tracking software that contains information that can be sorted and cross-referenced. These products are valued for what they do in terms of intellectual work, not in terms of what they would be worth if the silicon and plastic and glass and copper were sold on a commodities market. As for valuations, look at the valuations of companies like Dell, Microsoft, and Sun. Those valuations come nowhere near what they get were they to sell all their physical assets. In the past, the value of a company like Exxon or Ford was based on the company's fixed assets—buildings, production lines, vehicles, land. But today's companies are valued by the intellectual equity of the people who work there. Let's call this subset of the Information Revolution the Service Age, and it is in this Service Age that we have seen a marked transition from production jobs to service jobs. We have seen people moved from manipulating parts of machines and tools to manipulating abstract symbols—language, math, and computer code—and it is services now, not manufacturing, that is the principal path to creating value, efficiencies, and wealth in the world's most advanced economies. But the Information Revolution, driven by the information management made possible by the most so-phisticated intellectual products of the Service Age, is now enabling consumers to take the best of the Medieval and industrial ages, and meld them into an information- and technology-based economy that allows consumers to purchase custom products at mass-production prices, produced at mass-production speeds.

THE INTERACTIVE AGE

Computers have burst onto the world economic scene with all the glorious, positively disruptive power of a 1000-megaton bomb. There has been a realignment of power, wealth, and production easily as dramatic as that seen when the Industrial Revolution swept through Europe 250 years ago. Massive amounts of wealth have been concentrated in the hands of people who don't produce products you can feel and touch, but who produce great ideas. There has been a realignment of value, too. The assets of a company now are only minimally held in the "mortar and bricks" of the headquarters or corporate campus. The real value is the imaginative capacity of a company's workforce. Look at Microsoft, the last true software company. Its value as a company is not in the tangible things it produces (discs and CDs made of simple plastic), but in the intangible product of the workers' imaginations that adds value to that company, and, something that will become of paramount importance in the interactive marketplace, in the community that Microsoft users create through their use of common products. So you see that we have shifted our very understanding of value, from an emphasis on material value to an emphasis on intellectual and informational value, from the tangible to the intangible. See Figure 1–2.

Figure 1–2   Almost 50 percent of U.S. households have online connections either at home or at work. About 20 percent of households have purchased online, and that figure nearly doubled from a year ago.

What's perhaps most interesting is that the Information Revolution didn't just spring full-blown all on its own. Like any truly powerful force, it didn't just come out of nowhere. It is really the logical extension of all the economic activity that has come before it, as each economic era has incorporated all the lessons learned from all the previous economic eras. Only now, they have been supercharged and accelerated by technology, and it looks quite plainly as though the Information Revolution—for the first time in economic history—has the tools to "cherry pick" through the ages, gathering up only the very best aspects of all the economic eras that have come before it so they can be placed at the feet of the consumer. To help you see this more clearly and appraise the implications of this change, let me walk you through a syllogism, an argument of sort, with a couple of recent "givens."

The first given is that computers can store and process practically limitless amounts of information, enabling them to keep track of a limitless number of customers, yet still treat each one on an individual basis. The second given is that nearly any means of production of services or products can now be tied to computers and precisely controlled in a highly sophisticated way, where any product or service that is created can be customized at (or near) mass-production speed and price. The result: It is now possible to take the mass-production principles of the Industrial Revolution and marry them with informationally sophisticated computers in a way that allows the creation of products that are customized for each consumer, no matter how many customers there are, no matter how many producers and vendors there are, no matter how many changes are made from one product to the next, and no matter how many times this process is performed. Often this can happen during the actual production process. Even better, we are seeing that this information need not be transferred through laborious exchanges of mail, phone messages, faxes, and written documents, but it can be automated so that computers can talk to one another, and exchange pertinent information with little or no input from humans.

This type of information exchange and the ability to tie it to the means of production is nothing short of revolutionary, because as it is put into practice it inverts one of the most enduring maxims of economics. We are seeing the shift in control over the configuration of products and services *from* the producer of goods and services *to* the individual consumer (something we will examine in detail later in this book). This shift in control is possible only because computers are able to engage in highly innovative interactive data sharing that assembles and categorizes information in a highly sophisticated, integrated way and ties it to the means of production. That level of information management is necessary, because in order for producers of products and services to respond and communicate to individual customers in a one-to-one way, they have to have at hand sophisticated customer profiles, and they must be able to link these profiles seamlessly, integrally to both the means of production and the delivery of products and services.

Who will supply this crucial customer profile information and how will it be gathered? It will be supplied, always with the customer's permission, directly from the customer. And it will be gathered through monitoring and harvesting of the economic exchanges that make up the everyday transactions of people and businesses (e.g., interactive ordering, buying trends, replenishment schedules). As it is gathered, it will be organized in such a way that vendors, even vendors who have never met the customer, will be able to *predict customers' needs*. And even more than that, this information can be shared (with permission) in mutually beneficial alliances among companies that, before the age of interactivity, may have been natural enemies who competed fiercely. (This is something that is covered in later chapters of this book when we look at vortex-based allied consortiums, customer-created monopolies, and "co-opetition" alliances, which are a healthy combination of cooperation and competition.)

The sum total of these features of e-business is something I call the interactive marketplace, and what it offers is something that is both entirely new and as old as the hills. It has taken the

most desirable aspects of all past economic exchange (one-to-
one individualized service, craftsperson-quality customized goods,
vendors informed, often *automatically*, about their customers'
current and future needs) and combined them with product-manu-
facture and service-assembly systems that rely on mass-production principles informationally driven by state-of-the-art
computers. Those computers, in turn, integrally link individual
customer's requests to both the means of production and the delivery systems for those products and services, so that the resulting products are individually created and custom-delivered on a
one-to-one basis. See Figure 1–3.

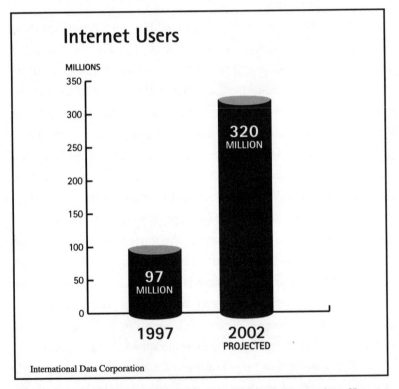

Figure 1–3   International Data Corporation estimates that the number of Internet
users will grow from 97 million at the end of 1998 to 320 million by 2002.

What's the sum total of these dramatic changes and the rise of interactivity? As you will read, it's nothing short of a bountiful economic future, one where customers interact integrally with product and service providers who work in open, mutually beneficial—not closed and adversarial—arrangements based first and foremost on individual customer service. This constitutes an epic economic realignment of resources and an inversion of traditional power paradigms. And in this book, I will teach you how to take full advantage of what's on the horizon—and *beyond the horizon*—of this new interactive marketplace as it is supercharged by the tools of the Information Revolution.

A "BRAVE NEW WORLD"? A "1984"?

If computers can keep such careful track of customers, wrest control of mass production, mass-customize products, and, as I have claimed, enable the personalized one-to-one service we saw in small-scale, craftsperson-based economies, then won't computers entirely control our lives? If computers *can* predict needs and actually predict the type of products or just-in-time service customers want before they even know they want them, then aren't we one step away from computers taking over our lives and *dictating* what we want and when?

These are good questions and they naturally arise whenever anyone starts to talk about an interactive marketplace, where custom products are produced on a single-customer by single-customer basis, using customer profiling. But the fear of computers controlling you is entirely unfounded. In fact, the control of all economic activity is going to switch from the producers of products and services, where it is now used abusively, to the consumers of those products and services. That's right, the consumer is in control, not only of the product and service production and delivery, but in direct control of all the information generated as a result of engaging in economic activity; in control enough to distribute it or withdraw it with the click of a mouse, unlike the way your personal information is distributed today for the profit of others.

This new interactive economic age is a world in which we can all be proud to live and raise our children, with economic parity across race and ethnic lines, a world based on transparent economic exchange, where each step in the production of and payment for a product is open for inspection by the consumer. This is a world where waste is minimized, because products will be highly targeted, not shot-gunned out into the world in the hopes someone will buy some of them. Efficiencies will be created by reducing redundant information processing and by creating products and services on an individualized just-in-time basis. This is a world where junk mail is a thing of the past, and all those trees that were felled for paper pulp won't be necessary. This is a world where advertising won't have to appeal to so many people to lure the few it really wants to reach. And the reason is because the same computers and technology that allow us to control machines, track information, and customize products can also be used just as effectively to control access to information, locking it down, and limiting it to just the people you want to see it. Not a single byte of data will go out without your permission, and if it does, it will be highly traceable, so the person who made an unauthorized release can be held liable. Information about your preferences for products and services will exist only with vendors that you choose. In the same way that you will have supreme control over the production of goods and services and the ability to customize them, you will have equally supreme control over who sees information about you, and how it is used. As discussed later in this book, the efficiencies created by these phenomena will cause an economic boom, an increase in everyone's wealth, and a rise in disposable income—all of which will drive the interactive marketplace further and faster.

Subsequent chapters of this book explain in-depth how this customer-controlled, interactive marketplace will become the dominant economic paradigm for all economic activity. I have provided a road map for anyone interested either in setting up an interactive business or for those investors and spectators seeking valuation metrics for companies that are attempting to attain this kind of information independence and control. You'll also find many examples of the sure emergence and demonstrated success of early efforts in the interactive marketplace in everything from pharmaceuticals and gourmet food to vitamins and even mass-produced, one-of-a-kind cars and computers. These examples will help you find ways of implementing this into your own e-business strategy.

C H A P T E R

Being Controlled

EXECUTIVE SUMMARY

Like it or not, if you're a consumer of almost any product, you've been controlled and directed by manufacturers, salespeople, tradespeople, and service people who have found it more profitable to limit the choice of products and prices than to offer a range of potentially lower-cost customizable items. This has been true for all products, from your everyday purchases, like lamp fixtures, cordless phones, and stereo speakers, to big-ticket items like boats, cars, and houses. In fact, the bigger the price tag, the less control consumers had and the more consumers have been directed, however subtly, as to what to buy. Why? Until recently, the means of production and sale of almost any item has been stuck in an antiquated, precomputer, Industrial Age mindset that makes it more profitable to offer fixed-price stock items instead of custom ones.

If by chance you have been able to exert some control over the design and assembly of products, you've very likely found that the means of production and the manufacturer's ability to predict precise costs have been so inflexible that your wishes could be fulfilled only at a greater cost and with inevitable delays, excuses, and cries of "yeah, we can do that, but it'll cost you a fortune." But now, in an epic shift brought on by the Information Revolution, customers increasingly find they are in complete control, as sophisticated software, powerful computers, and lightning-fast delivery of perfect just-in-time information can break down and precisely track ("proceduralize") all the steps to even highly complicated processes like building a car or house, and give consumers a chance to influence that process directly. Customers will soon be able to fully customize one-of-a-kind products at the same (or lower) cost than stock items. Even better, procedural-based systems integrated with a calendar program, can be infinitely flexible, enabling changes of nearly any magnitude at any point in the construction or assembly process. Consequently, consumers will soon be able to control every aspect of the design, assembly, compilation, building, management, and maintenance of anything they buy. If you're a customer, are you ready to take control? If you're a service provider or manufacturer, are you ready to hand that control over? You'd better be, because customer control is to be embraced, not feared. Indeed, it will be an integral part of all future commerce.

ARE YOU BEING CONTROLLED?

Any honest critique of the technological state of today's economy—for all its strengths and dynamism—has to recognize that, sadly, the customer is rarely in command of his or her buying decisions. Sure, some vendors have given over limited control, and others have given enough control for customers to be, if not convinced, then at least kept at bay with a feeling that they have a say in the manufacture, construction, and assembly of what they are buying. But in all truth, no matter what sector of the economy you look at, there is a limited number of types of products, consumer goods, and services available, and consumers are steered to pick from that limited selection. Whether it's cars, houses, computers, or stereos, the selection is essentially limited. If it's not strictly limited, it is at least uncustomizable (or customizable only at great expense). The same is true for services like banking, health care, and house maintenance. And a case could easily be made that this is true for media, books, magazines, and even education. When you go shopping for any of these services, you get to "walk the aisles," so to speak, but ultimately you are forced to pick from a selection of stock items. Oh, the selection may be expansive—like that found for books—but you are really limited to what others have determined you want, without having given you much of a chance to intervene during the creation of the product or service that you purchase. Walk the aisles of Wal-Mart, America's premiere retailer (or visit their Web page). You don't get to customize the products you are about to purchase. You get to choose from among stock offerings. Unhappy with the color of the umbrellas for sale? The patterns on a plate set? The arrangement of windows on that back-packing tent? Well, you've had no real say in how those products were created. So, you're essentially guided by a lack of choice into picking from something you would have changed had you been given the chance. This is true not just at Wal-Mart, but at the vast number of retailers out there, whether it's JC Penney's, Gap and Banana Republic, or LL Bean. It's just the way business gets done, because it's the most profitable way to sell affordable items; customization has been too costly and too hard to control, and frankly the consumer hasn't barked too loudly about the status quo. I realize that in the United States, a country driven by the freedom of choice and the "magic of the marketplace," this sounds like heresy, but it's true. Why? Simple: Until the relatively recent advent of computers that can be integrally tied to the mass production process (more on that in Chapter 4), it has been cheaper for manufacturers to make and sell stock products than to go to the trouble of creating each one custom. This has served as a powerful motivation for companies to spend oodles of advertising dollars to convince you that stock products are what you really want to buy.

But now we are seeing that technology is rewriting the rules of interaction between the consumer and the producer of a product or service; our economy is becoming *interactive*. The consumer-to-provider relationship is changing at an exponentially increasing rate, as one dynamic computer innovation piles upon another. These innovations are brought on by integrated, Internet-enabled systems that allow the computers of customers and businesses to talk to one another and exchange information in an automated way. These days, this is what is commonly called business-to-business transactions, or B2B. As explained in the introduction, a B2B system is a data translation or data mapping protocol that lets different computer platforms talk to one another in very smart ways. Information is automatically exchanged across these platforms based on events in the world. For instance, there are now available commercial refrigerators that have barcode scanners on their doors. When a restaurant worker removes a food item and wants the supply chain to replenish it, he or she scans the bar code at the door. Immediately, the supplier of that food item is alerted to the need to replenish that item in that restaurant, with the information required for delivery and payment already programmed in the system. The information moves across computer platforms and "populates" the computer systems of those pertinent links in the supply chain. No one has to call in an order or fax a list of food items. The information exchange is a seamless, B2B transaction, even though it is focused just on one type of item: food. See Figure 2–1.

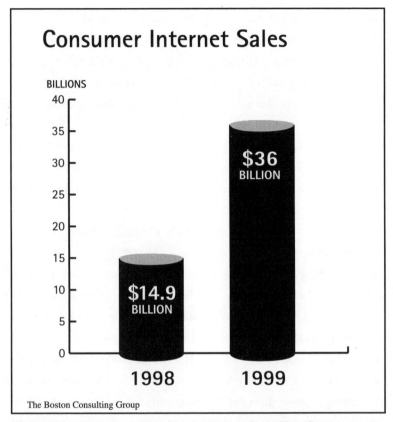

Figure 2–1   A study conducted by the Boston Consulting Group says consumer Internet sales will leap from $14.9 billion in 1998 to $36 billion in 1999.

Let's ratchet this example up a notch or two, as we move toward true interactivity. When you purchase a product at Wal-Mart, and you pay for the item, the Wal-Mart supply chain is instantly fully aware of that purchase. The supply chain is also aware of how many of those items are missing from the shelves and when to begin replenishing those items so the shelves remain full. The information flows across the inventory and accounting systems of the various links in the supply chain and populates the inventory and accounting systems of the product suppliers. Now, we still haven't moved into full configuration management with the Wal-Mart model, but Wal-Mart has fully automated its own supply chain with a truly efficient and highly profitable automation of information for delivery of a wide range of stock products.

Now apply these two examples to a custom configuration model based on these B2B principles. When you use the Internet to configure and purchase a Dell computer, you interact with a Web page to log in your request for computer features. That information is distributed automatically to the various links in the supply chain that feed the computer assembly line where your computer will be pieced together. No human intervention is required for this information to be dispersed. It is exchanged, in and out of the Dell system, across computer platforms, in an automated fashion based on what the consumer ordered. In the Dell model, the B2B backbone allows the consumer to intervene in the design of the product he or she will consume. This is a highly profitable, working model of a B2C system based on B2B principles that can deliver one-to-one, custom-configured products for cheaper than the cost of comparable stock products on the shelves in nearby stores. In various stages of development and maturity, using these models, the customer can express a need (often through an electronic message that can be triggered automatically by calendar events) and let the computers of pertinent businesses swap information and work out the production and delivery details amongst themselves. Even better, this interactive consumer-friendly system is capable of processing and precisely aiming this information at various steps in the manufacture and delivery of nearly any consumer good, so it can be customized and changed *even as it is being assembled.*

These technological advances—the screaming edge of the interactive marketplace—have presented us all with a startling dynamic. Customers are now beginning to take commanding control of the design, manufacture (or assembly and composition), and delivery of some of the items they buy. They are customizing them, often through automated, integrated configuration systems tied directly to the modes of production and to delivery and inventory systems. Soon, customers will be exerting this control over *all* of the items they buy, from groceries and car-repair services, to stereos, music CDs, appliances, and even the construction of custom houses and custom cars. This is more than customers taking just some control over just a few aspects of the creation of what they buy, like color, system configuration, and motor size. This is more about the customer taking control of every single buying and design decision, while having full access to design options, pricing, component inventory, and production scheduling through transparent integrated systems. These systems will be open for inspection, changes, updates, alterations, and reorganization at any time. (Customers will not have to become engineers, industrial designers, and architects to participate in this way, as you will see in the "configuration management" discussion later in this chapter.)

In the past, manufacturers limited consumers' control over design options and price choices. This was either to ensure their profitability by cutting down the learning curve of the creation or installation of the product and service, or because they simply were lazy. But now consumers are gaining that control through online resources that can instantly search for alternative products and prices. It's increasingly easy to shop around. If you are on Amazon.com and you would like to see the cost of the book you are interested in at another competing site, it's easy to click your mouse and take a look. Buy.com is so confident of their prices that they actually do this work for you, by putting up their competitors' costs side by side with their price. By hyperlinking from site to site, with the click of a mouse, consumers can compare vendor prices across town as easily as they can across the country. That's what we call *low switching costs*, and you will see throughout this book that Internet-enabled low switching costs are having a profound effect on how products are produced, bundled, and priced. See Figure 2–2.

Is your company ready to accommodate and profit in this economic world that works at light speed and has none of the

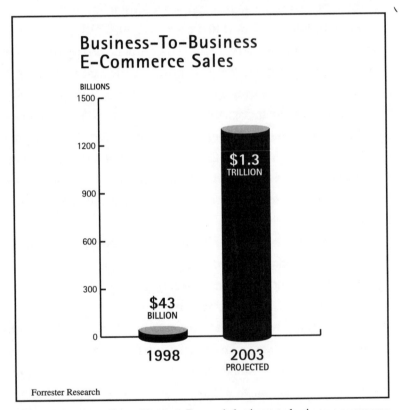

Figure 2–2   According to Forrester Research, business-to-business e-commerce is expected to grow from $43 billion in 1998 to $1.3 trillion in 2003, accounting for more than 90 percent of the dollar value of e-commerce in the United States by 2003.

walls and barriers the old-fashioned economy put between the customer and the limitless choices open to them? If not, you'd better think of retooling to make your company interactive and e-business–enabled. The first step to take is to recognize that your business plan must accommodate the fact that barriers no longer exist and switching costs will only go down as technology improves. Businesses that depend only on a technology solution to offer a wider selection of inexpensive products than their competitor will soon find someone else coming in with better technology to take the market share away from them. The answer, as this book argues throughout and as the final chapter explicitly explains, is *community* not technology. By generating a true community at your site or virtual place of business (or using technology to reach out to existing communities to enable seamless exchange), you engage consumers in something more than a hit-and-run selling and buying experience; you interweave them in the data protocols of your system, and vest them in increasingly robust customer profiles that allied vendors can use to deliver highly targeted, value-added products and services across a wider range of options.

DO YOU DOUBT THE FUTURE?

Some doubt this notion of complete customer control in an interactive marketplace. Generally, people don't doubt that customers want this control. After all, who wouldn't want to design and personalize nearly everything they buy? The will of the consumers is clear. They want the control. What people doubt is that the technology exists to accommodate this control. If it does—and it does, I can assure you—then the only remaining obstacle is for the manufacturers and vendors of products and services to come on board and freely offer this control to their customers. Once that happens—and it is beginning to happen now—then customers will soon be demanding this type of interactive service and accepting no substitute.

In this chapter, I want simply to lay out the problem of where the economy has gone wrong, why customers have been controlled, and how Internet-enabled integrated e-business systems hold a solution. To help make my case, I also want to compare two manufacturing processes—car assembly and house building—to see how the interactive marketplace is changing them and show examples of how the interactive marketplace will soon change *all* manufacture and assembly of products and services. I have chosen to look at car assembly because it is a proceduralized process that is ripe for configuration management, customization, and complete customer control. In comparison, house building represents one of the most unruly and untamable processes in our economy, a process prone to spinning out of control, especially as houses move increasingly toward individual custom designs. If we can figure out how to tame these processes, open them up to customer-controlled customization through integrated, Internet-enabled, interactive e-business systems, then we can tame and control just about any process. Now let's take a closer look.

THE PROCEDURAL APPROACH— LACKING CUSTOMIZABILITY

Assembling a car from its "kit of parts" presents far fewer challenges to assembly line workers than does the assembly of a house from its kit of parts. When you build a car, you have a conveyor belt that moves the car's chassis along, stabilizing it for robotic arms to make precise welds. The various parts that are installed— headlights, fenders, door locks, seats—are at-the-ready and pre-tested. There is little or no "learning curve," because the installer does the same exact task over and over again, and it is the only task he or she performs. Even better, from a quality-control manager's point of view, the car is assembled in a predictable, linear sequence, from the installation of the axles to the application of roof paint. Training and overseeing workers may present a challenge, but it is an easily surmountable one. Workers can all be trained to a high degree of effectiveness because the same company employs them all. Technological updates, design changes, or changes to the car building process can be readily incorporated. With proper management, each worker stands ready at his station with a clear idea of what his job is.

Controlling the work site environment in a car factory doesn't present any problems. Weather? It doesn't matter. Come rain or snow, the conditions inside the car plant are always ideal for building cars. Nighttime? Daytime? That doesn't matter either. You can run three crews on three shifts, no matter where the sun or moon is in the sky. In short, the assembly process is highly controllable.

Predicting costs for a process like this is relatively easy. Since the car has been preassembled on a computer, or is comprised of components that can be individually priced out, it's relatively easy for computer systems to predict how much the car will cost, long before it is built. You price each component, and add those costs together to obtain the total material cost. You price out your labor by adding up units of work expended. This is a relatively straightforward calculation, because the same tasks are repeated over and over again, day after day. Add the material and labor costs together, and you have your total hard costs for the car. It's fairly easy to calculate what percent profit you add to that hard-cost figure. Even better, this job costing for car assembly is so carefully controlled and easy to monitor, you can easily pick out cost errors. If there is a cost error on the first car, it can be accounted for on the second car and incorporated into the price of every car after that, as the system is fine-tuned.

What makes all this possible is recognizing that the product is a kit of parts and the assembly follows a critical path, which is essentially a linear timeline that defines which steps must be taken in what order. Once you realize that fact, you can break the process down to its component steps and carefully plan and monitor those steps with clever computer systems. With this approach, you can even take lessons learned and figures derived from one type of car and use them on another type of car by moving exact unit costs and highly refined labor estimates from one assembly model to another.

For all its positive attributes, there is only one problem with car assembly. The system cannot accommodate changes from one car to another. If a custom order came in, the assembly line, with all its predictability, would fall apart trying to accommodate a single change. So, with car assembly, we have predictable costs, labor, and price, but we sacrifice customizability.

THE MASS-PRODUCED, "AFTER-THE-FACT" APPROACH

Like car assembly, building a house is just an assembly of a kit of parts. But unlike car assembly, building a house is a chaotic process. The kit of parts has (until the advent of computers) been hard to proceduralize and the assembly process hard to track. With home building and car assembly, the same number of people are involved (around 80 per unit), but instead of headlight installers and engine builders, you have carpenters, plumbers, tilers, and roofers, many of whom are hard to control because they work for different companies. As for components, you've got the same number, around 40,000. But instead of assembling these components from a conveyor belt, the builder assembles the house outside in all kinds of weather. Unlike the car-building process, where the parts are neatly arranged, the parts for a house are shipped on trucks from all over the map and are often delivered to a pile of dirt.

Can you imagine if autoworkers had to assemble a car this way? Go ahead, stick 80 people in a vacant lot with the engineering diagram of a car. Dump 40,000 components on them in a hodge-podge way, with deliveries that are hard to time properly, and ask them to build a car. No wonder home building has such a high dropout rate. Companies just can't process the information fast enough to stay in business.

The result of all this is that contractors try to control the customers since they can't control the job. Contractors, like car makers, can find stability and predictability only by producing the same product over and over again. I'm sure that if you sat down with a contractor and spoke frankly, he would freely admit that, like car makers, he has used his marketing and persuasion skills to convince the consumer that the product he knows how to produce profitably, the stock product, is the one they want to buy. But unlike the car maker, the builder gets pressure from his clients to customize the product. (This pressure is increasing dramatically in the Information Age, as most houses are going custom.) He agrees to customize the product—he needs the work—and figures he'll determine how to price out and organize the job once he gets underway. Unfortunately, this leads to problems, because most builders are ill equipped to handle custom configuration of every house they build. They end up giving more and more creative excuses for lost time, unwieldy accounting, and inflexible work crews that seem incapable of accommodating even the simplest design or schedule change once the building process gets underway. In short, he ends up trying to control the customer because he can't control the product.

The problem is that most houses are built, like so many other manufactured products in our economy, with "after-the-fact" job costing and inflexible, unwieldy production techniques. The after-the-fact job costing means that the true cost of a product cannot be predicted until the end, when the builder can add up all he has spent. In all truth, he can only confidently, profitably build his houses when he produces the same product over and over again, like a car maker.

CUSTOMIZABLE PROCEDURALIZED SYSTEMS

Given this set of problems, can we find a solution that will accommodate all industries and all customers? Yes. The solution can be found in integrated configuration and procedural-based systems. Car building and house building are good case studies for explaining how this approach can work in the interactive marketplace to deliver what the customer wants. That's because integrated configuration and procedural-based systems, and the management approach they embody, can be adapted to any other industry. When implemented, they can turn unruly, unpredictable processes and closed systems into open-system, critical-path-managed, predictable processes. Currently, consumers can buy houses that, for the right price, can be customized (size, room configuration, siding, color, window and door placement, roof type, etc.), but that customization comes at the cost of an uncontrollable schedule and a wildly fluid price. With cars, you are offered a firm price and delivery date, but it comes at the cost of customizable features. You are essentially offered stock models on a take-it-or-leave-it basis. But when you have open-system, critical-path-managed processes, you have all the advantages of both these product assembly systems, with none of the drawbacks. You get the labor cost, precise completion date, and price predictability of the car assembly line, and the customizability of the house-building process. From the consumers' perspective, they too are offered the best of all worlds: control, customizability, precise delivery dates, and a firm price—all written into the contract before the first construction or assembly step is taken.

Let's look at how the proceduralized approach works. But before we apply this theoretically to the home-building or car-assembly processes, let's look at where the procedural approach is already working with wild success in today's economy. McDonald's, the most successful franchise in the world, has 25,000 stores. Yet how do you think they can run each of these with such efficiency? How can they assure the buyers of these franchises that they will make a profit? And how can they hire such a largely unskilled, often transitory, workforce and still run a high-tech operation with such predictability? *They proceduralized it.* McDonald's knows how long each French fry should be cooked, how hot the oil temperature should be, how much salt should be on the finished product, and exactly how many units of each product should be used during the course of the day. Because they know the cooking and delivery procedure so well—and have tweaked it by monitoring any variances from the procedure—you get the same product no matter what McDonald's you go to anywhere in the world. McDonald's has even calculated the exact difference between a regular order of fries and a "super-sized" order: thirteen. Business owners across the world would love to be this knowledgeable about their businesses. How did they do it? McDonald's studied the process of cooking fast food and broke it down into its component steps. It placed those steps on a critical path, and then monitored the execution of it. Where the fries came out overcooked, they tweaked the cooking time by shortening it; where the fries came out too limp, they lengthened that cooking cycle. If cooked or uncooked fries went to waste one Friday afternoon because too much was taken out of the freezer, that waste factor was incorporated into the procedure for all Friday afternoons, and incorporated into the procedures at all future McDonald's stores with similar demographics. McDonald's gathered all this knowledge and wrote it into a procedure to be used everywhere. They update it still and are continually hammering out all the kinks and inefficiencies in the system. When a company is working with systems in this procedural fashion, they find that the time they used to spend putting out fires can instead be used to search for even more efficiency.

This style of information management quickly leads to a stage where a process is tracked so closely that you start to look just at where events varied from your predictions; you look just at the exceptions. This "managing by exception" is a premiere example of why the procedural system works so well, because changes in the critical path can be incorporated to increase the efficiency of that (or similar) critical path every time it is subsequently run.

The result? McDonald's is able to predict cost, labor, and

inventory with real precision. And lest we forget that this is all in service of the customer: Everyone shopping at any McDonald's gets a seriously consistent product. You can go to a McDonald's anywhere in the United States and eat food that tastes exactly the same, whether it's in Durham, North Carolina, Berkeley, California, or Burlington, Vermont.

By taking complicated processes like car building and house building, breaking them into their procedural steps, and tracking those steps through a critical path approach, you have proceduralized those systems just as you have the cooking of food at McDonald's. Plus, by opening those systems up to customer influence, you make them customizable. Next, let's e-business–enable these systems. Let's link the customer interactively to the production and delivery of the product. By doing so, you enable the flow of information between the customer and the product-assembly system. In its most rudimentary form, this is when a customer goes on a Web page and configures a product he is about to purchase by mixing and matching qualities with the click of a mouse. At a higher level, this is when one computer talks to other linked computers and together—with very little human input—these systems share resources and work together to predict and deliver just-in-time products that consumers need. Systems like these can also be enabled to respond to information that is exchanged from computer to computer simply because consumers have manipulated an icon or picture to express their desires, as when the customer is linked to a configuration-managed, procedural-based integrated system.

This interactive e-business notion of handing over control of a product or service's creation to the consumer may make some people's hearts skip a beat. But the shift in control we're discussing—and this shift is happening everywhere in the emerging interactive economy—will be welcomed by everyone involved in the process. As you continue reading, you will discover how this shift in control will be painless and how companies that *don't* accommodate customer control of configuration-managed, pro-cedural-based integrated systems will be run out of business by forward-thinking companies that welcome the customer as a fully empowered partner.

CONFIGURATION MANAGEMENT AND CUSTOMIZABILITY

As previously mentioned, the ability to take a procedural approach and apply it to the control of nearly any process rests on the rec-ognition that before anything is built—a house, a car, a copier machine, a guitar, anything at all—it is a kit of parts. Once you recognize that fact and simultaneously see that, given the capaci-ties of a computer, a kit containing four parts is just as easy to proceduralize and control as a kit containing 80,000 parts, you will see the boundless potential that proceduralizing has not only for the assembly and customizing of products but also for the handing over of control of that assembly to anyone who wants (and deserves or pays to have) it. It is no more difficult for a computer to store, recall, implement and track a single, limited step-by-step critical path process than it is for it to store, recall, implement and track an expansive critical path with 1000 or 10,000 steps. What's more, a computer can store, recall, implement, and track these change *during* the manufacturing or assembly pro-cess in response to changes made *while the process is underway.*

Yet, if we make this many design choices available to the consumer, with so many consequent critical paths that could

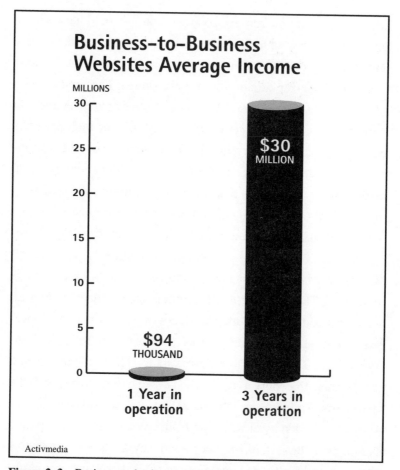

Figure 2–3 Business-to-business web sites have flourished recently, as business planners realize that the real savings are in data mapping their business processes directly to other business processes.

change as the consumer configures and reconfigures the product (either before or during the construction or assembly), how can these changes be managed without demanding that the consumer become a computer scientist or engineer? After all, it may not make much of a difference to the overall product design if you change its color (e.g., changing a room from beige to Navaho white, or a car color from red to green), but it would have a huge impact if you started letting consumers change the product's size and structural configuration (as when a wall is moved a few feet, or a roof changes pitch, or you drop in side air bags and a moon roof on your car). And since the proceduralized management of a project grants the consumer access to customizing their products before and during their creation, we must somehow offer an interface that consumers can effortlessly use. This configuration method must not require that the customer master the engineering required to make the desired change, and it must allow the builder/manufacturer to automate the integration of rapidly changing information back into every aspect of their system with high efficiency, whether the system has three weeks or three seconds to respond. That's where "configuration management" comes in.

First, a definition: Integrated, configuration-managed, procedural-based systems are systems that can be controlled by configuring the actual product being made. They are based on a step-by-step procedure as it is broken down based on the product's kit of parts. And they are integrated because they disperse the information needed by or resulting from any changes and populate it throughout the system, in a very smart way. Let's break down this long term and look at each word. *Integrated.* If you use a program like *Quicken®* or *TurboTax®*, you are using an integrated system. These are systems that take one-time entry of information and disperse it anywhere it is required. Enter the cost of medical care in one data field, and the integrated program sends that to other data fields for other calculations. More sophisticated integrated systems can strip information off of a graphic or image and send it to fabrication tools, as you will see in an example below. *Configuration managed.* These are systems that are graphic-, image- or object-based tools that allow anyone to design a product. But they have embedded behind the lines of the image loads of data, lodged within an expert system that will disallow the impossible (say a clear span between car wheels of 14 feet; a cantilever that extends too far given the weight it is loaded with), as it allows the user to see the cost and material implications of their decisions. *Procedural-based.* This is the process of breaking down a multistep operation into its critical path. Earlier we referred to how your approach to building an item can change once you realize that all products are really just a kit of parts; well, the procedure is the proper order in which they must be assembled.

At its most basic level, configuration management is nothing more than a presentation of the options available for a product or service that are available to a consumer to customize a purchase. But behind the scenes of this presentation are thousands of lines of computer code that manage all the possible manufacturing or assembly paths that could result from a customer's choices, and any rules that might exclude certain choices when others are made. For example, in the near future, a CAD (computer-assisted design) representation of a house will be tied seamlessly to this configuration management process. The customer will start with a graphic of the house he wants to build, and select from various options that might change, like rooflines, windows, room configurations, etc. When he sits down at the CAD drawing, and makes these selections, he isn't interested in the design consequences of his actions. (And he shouldn't be. He just wants a nice custom home, and he doesn't want to learn architecture and building procedures to oversee its construction.) That CAD drawing can be integrated into every aspect of the building procedure, so that as the configuration changes, it updates every other aspect of the system. When the design is finalized, it notifies/updates anything and everyone affected by the changes, as it simultaneously updates the price. For instance, if the consumer adjusts the bedroom walls in CAD to make them five feet wider in each direction, the configuration change would instantly be reflected in the critical path required to build that room that way. Hence, the consequences of that change will be flushed through the system, as it updates the budget and the quantities for lumber, insulation, siding, roofing, and all material orders, work schedules, labor estimates, and subcontractors' specs. (The system might even be smart enough to limit the changes within preset structural parameters.) On the screen that the consumer is viewing, there easily can be a budget calculator that instantly totals up the cost implications of each change. The consumer could drag out the walls, making the room larger until they see the budget number on the screen match the budget number allotted in their checkbook. When the consumer arrives at a final design, the integrated system can reach out online to purchase and arrange for the just-in-time delivery of the goods required to fulfill the customer's expressed wishes. It does this by alerting, seamlessly, business-to-business, the various companies that must work together.

But what about configuration management once a job is underway? Given that the system is based on the critical path, it's just as easy to accommodate changes once a job gets underway as it is to accommodate changes before a job starts. If during the construction of the house, the customer walks through and sees something he'd like changed in an aspect of the structure that hasn't been built, he can manipulate the CAD representation of the house to make that change. The consequences aren't dire, as they might have been in past years, under older "after-the-fact" systems. The reason the change can be accommodated is that the integrated system is designed to flex in response to daily changes to the job, instantly notifying every part of the system and every player involved of the changes in a timely way, rearranging the steps in the critical path. If a customer sees that he wants tile rather than wood floors, he can drag and drop it in place on his computer screen. The material ordering and work stages change in response to this change. The same for changing wall finishes, cabinets, and—if it's early enough in the process—window and door placement, location of fixtures, even ceiling heights and roof pitches.

Though I have used house building and a CAD drawing to illustrate what configuration management is, it can be done with any manufacturing or service assembly process that is managed by critical-path-based integrated configuration and procedural-based management systems. It won't be long before you go to the car dealer, step up to a kiosk, and through dragging and dropping, assemble the features you would like to see in a new car. (You can already customize some car features now using early versions of this configuration-management system through the WebXchange system set up by Ford and Oracle that was announced in November 1999. GM and AOL have a similar arrangement; though after you custom configure your car, the system merely searches among stock products to see which one comes closest to your design.) And just as we saw in the CAD house configuration, you will be able to see the cost and design implications of your choices as you make them. The car industry is absolutely ripe for taking advantage of configuration-managed purchasing, because its assembly system is already so heavily proceduralized. It wouldn't take much more to enable the customization of each product as it moves down the production line (more on this in Chapter 4).

Does this sound like something that's too far into the future? It's not. In fact, you can already "configuration manage" some products you buy: airline tickets, custom-made vitamins, custom-made CDs, custom-made clothing or computers—all of these things can be purchased through the Internet after they have been assembled to your individual specifications. The customer may not be using a drag-and-drop graphic interface... yet. But it is coming soon. Once manufacturing or product and service assembly processes are proceduralized and automated—and many are now or are moving that way, *supercharged and accelerated* by integrated Internet-enabled software—the control that configuration management offers can be exercised as easily over the compilation of an $11 music CD as it is over a $111,000 house or a $111 million jetliner. That's because no matter what the size of the product, no matter how many steps it takes to complete it, we are always dealing with the critical path, which is nothing more than a step-by-step representation of the assembly of the product's kit of parts. The computer running the proceduralized system is just as confident accounting for the overall play-length of songs on a music CD as it is at accounting for the design implications of a customer dropping in a dozen skylights the day before the roof is being built. Again, this is not limited just to industries like home building, where the computer might know how big the rafters have to be to support a roof full of skylights. Look, for instance, at the way successful companies like Cisco Systems or Dell do business. A customer can go online to configure a system to his or her liking, and the online expert system interface works with the customer to design a system based on his or her expressed needs. The manufacturer adjusts their own critical paths in response to the customer's decisions, and reaches out to the supply chain (intra- and intercompany) to request parts based on real, not forecasted, demand. The manufacturer's expert interface can even optimize the customer's system in ways that he or she may not have thought of when they began the configuration process. Customers used to have to talk with an engineer or computer expert to configure these systems, but now that a computer knows all the design implications of every single change, they can just "talk" to a computer. Soon, customers will simply manipulate pictures, dragging and dropping icons, and the computers will talk to each other in the background to specify your product

The system configuration mentioned above is really just one more facet of interactive e-business. Businesses are using the power of computers to squeeze out inefficiencies and tighten up slack in the supply chain as they allow consumers direct control over the configuration of the products they will buy. Imagine a day—not far off—when these systems link together the entire chain of specific industries, on one integrated system. As orders are made using configuration management, the entire supply chain flexes to respond, as computers talk to one another, integrating and disseminating the information crucial to the fulfillment of a customer's order.

This approach already enables companies to sell custom products at the same cost or less than stock. In fact, Dell and Cisco are already able to charge less for a custom product than they do for a stock item. An off-the-shelf computer with the capacity and speed of, say, a Dell Latitude laptop would cost far more than the computer configured just for one consumer, who likely paid for it before or as it was being made. This is possible for a number of reasons. If Dell were to make stock computers and put them on the shelves, they would have to pay all the costs associated with warehouse and retail inventory, insurance, and carrying costs on the products as they waited for buyers. With all products custom—each configured for a known buyer, with each assembly based on a critical-path configuration—there are none of the traditional risks and costs of floating products out on the retail market. The examples of Dell and Cisco are already being carried into other industries, and—to continue with our examples—the car-building and house-building industries are soon to follow.

Another dynamic of the e-business economy is evident here too. When futurists talk of a world of e-business where all products are custom, and *all* customers are linked online to *all* their vendors, it is, clearly, years away. But that should not stop the astute businessperson from recognizing that these changes are imperative, that they are sure to come. E-business is happening now, all around us. In 1998, total e-business business-to-business sales (e.g., Dell, Cisco) reached $48 billion, dwarfing by 5 to 1 the gross total of *all* Web-based sales (e.g., Amazon.com, LandsEnd.com). By 2003, business-to-business sales will total at least $1.3 *trillion*, around one in ten dollars spent by U.S. businesses. You also see here that e-business will not swoop in and take over one fateful day. Instead, it will happen incrementally, wired to existing systems, with companies like Dell and Cisco leading the way, sorting out the good and bad methods for conducting e-business, with other forward-looking businesses following these "cowbell" companies and learning by their examples and profits.

THE CHANGING CUSTOMER

Do customers want this kind of control? Yes. That's because the computer capabilities of the interactive marketplace are changing and enabling the customer almost as much as they are changing the way we all engage in commerce. Whereas in the past it was "necessity is the mother of invention," now it is "invention is the mother of necessity." Once consumers see that products can be easily customized, they will all want to have this power as a necessary, integral part of their lives. Plus, quite frankly, it's not the 1950s, when neighborhoods of two or three hundred identical homes were built for America's burgeoning Middle Class and consumers didn't have a choice. These days, buyers of cars, computers, paint, and furniture are after differentiation and individualism, and they are not likely to want to buy products just like their neighbors' After all, wouldn't that be a boring future? If we had only as many dress or suit patterns as we have stock house plans, wouldn't it be a bore to walk around town and see the same 20 suits, the same 20 pairs of shoes or the same 20 dresses? And yet we have tolerated this in the design and building of homes.

These days, buyers are astute, educated, technologically savvy people who know quality when they see it. Technology and the dispersal of information through a wide variety of media, traditional and nontraditional, have taken huge steps toward making the buying process transparent and multisourced, with every aspect increasingly open to competition and the questioning gaze of consumers eager to save money and to find something original. These same customers will demand to know the *full range* of design and material and with the Internet as the shopper's ultimate search tool, they have considerable latitude when looking for what they want, no matter where it is made and sold. In short, consumers are increasingly able to do an end-run of what were considered privileged sources of information about products and design. For example, with switching costs so low, it's as easy as clicking a mouse to view any number of, say, houseware manufacturers' offerings, whether your contractor or local supply house carry that line or not. The result? The tables have been turned, and service and product providers are now confronted with customers who may be more knowledgeable about material and design options than they are!

Design selection is changing too. In the past, the majority of products were of stock designs, but now we are seeing an increasing number of custom offerings, without that much of an increase in cost (manufacturers are taking advantage of this same technology that consumers can now have access to). Clearly the ground is shifting beneath the feet of manufacturers who used to create stock designs over and over again, making a profit because they knew exactly what their costs were, based on historical data. These days, customers are, or will soon be, designing their own products using easy-to-use, off-the-shelf software, sometimes supplied by the manufacturer, who, truth be known, looks forward to the cost-saving prospect of being able to integrate consumer-source product specs, if they can be pulled right into the manufacturing process without delaying production. With a dynamic like this at work, if a manufacturer or supplier can't confidently and quickly accommodate a custom design and price it out accurately, the customer will move on to a manufacturer or supplier who can.

If you are a product or service provider, are you prepared to deal with complete customer control and are you aware of the e-business tools available for you to take up this challenge? This is not something out of *Star Trek* or *Terminator II*. This is a technology that is rushing headlong at us, and it will be the dominant mode of commercial interaction in the foreseeable future. Prepare yourself. And profit.

THE RULES ARE REWRITTEN

The rules of interaction among the consumer, manufacturer, and the homebuilder are being entirely rewritten by technology, as they are adopting the very best features from the worlds of mass production, customizability, connectivity, and e-business. These technological changes and enhanced capabilities are coming forth at an unprecedented rate of speed, with wave after wave of innovation brought on by computers and the Information Revolution. Technologies only dreamed of ten years ago are now becoming commonplace. Highly refined, highly targeted information is increasingly available effortlessly to anyone with a computer. Sophisticated software—the integrated configuration and procedural-based project management software mentioned earlier—that tracks and precisely controls a nearly infinite number of steps in a job of almost any level of complexity are increasingly common and affordable. The home-building industry used as an example above is just a metaphor, an "acid test," that proves that if this unruly process can be tamed by interactivity and configuration-managed, procedural-based systems that borrow the best of all earlier economic systems, then any process in nearly any industry can be tamed, mastered, and controlled. This will come in part through consumers' access to the Internet and their increasing comfort with the interactive marketplace. But the software for such detailed, integrated manipulation of the information required for designing, pricing and building large-scale or complicated products will come from the most unlikely source: the builders, the manufacturers, the vendors, the service providers. And they will be giving this control away, willingly. Why? They will be benefiting from the customers' total control, as they supply customers with materials, products, and services using computer and information-delivery systems that are highly flexible and fully integrated into every aspect of job costing and schedule. This will put an end once and for all to the inherently manipulative process that everyone willingly entered, but nobody ever wanted to be part of, where excuses and compartmentalizing the customer were essential to success and profit.

C H A P T E R

One-to-One Marketing, One-to-One Service

EXECUTIVE SUMMARY

Computers may not be as smart as humans, but what they can do—track and organize a nearly infinite number of moving pieces—they do flawlessly, with unlimited memory and perfect, instant recall. Using this power, today's computers are revolutionizing a unique form of interactive commerce that is individualizing and automating the economic and information exchange that businesses now experience on a mass-market basis. Using the ever-expanding Internet, increasingly high-speed data transmission, and clever software, a company's computers can now: 1) tell customers apart using in-depth customer profiles, no matter how many customers they deal with; 2) interact instantly with customers while providing one-to-one service, as though that customer's daily needs were the sole focus of the entire company's attention; and 3) respond, one-to-one, to a customer's service and product needs by using his or her individual input—linked through e-business computer-to-computer exchanges of informa-

tion—to customize the delivery of a service or product, or the custom manufacture of one-of-a-kind products.

The implications of these three capacities are earth-shaking and they are already causing a seismic shift in the world of commerce, even in their fledgling states. Software and computer technology available today (through products like Broad Vision or I2) are able to greatly enhance any company's ability to interact with customers on a one-to-one basis with enough flexibility to enable just-in-time delivery of individualized products, services, and information. Through profiling, software can even accurately predict future individual needs in a way that greatly enhances customer loyalty, which itself increasingly becomes an effortless result of the one-to-one approach. In fact, when using a one-to-one approach, profits actually rise with the amount of services delivered, because for repeat customers providing for their every need requires less effort to maintain higher levels of service, and that service can often be delivered automatically.

One-size-fits-all, mass-market, mass-production companies that use inflexible means of production that do not welcome customers' ongoing input, or that have no ability to track, recall, and integrate a customer's needs into the delivery of future custom services are already withering, as one-to-one companies flourish on the basis of their ability to service customers with tailor-made, flexible, highly responsive, individualized, attentive service or product assembly, delivered within an economy unheard of even five years ago.

ONE-TO-ONE MARKETING, ONE-TO-ONE SERVICE

The last chapter looked at how the rules are being rewritten and customers are finding themselves—through the aid of computer technology and increasingly automated exchanges of information—in control of all the decisions around the design and construction of nearly any product they purchase. It's a complete reversal of the traditional producer-customer relationship, where producers used to control all the decisions, even limiting options that they weren't familiar with or couldn't confidently provide at a profit. This shift to customer control and customization is a paradigm for all future commerce in the interactive marketplace. Yet even as this procedural approach gives customers commanding control over the manufacturing, assembly, or construction process, it is also inherently flexible, unlike the rather rigid management "systems" (if you can call them that) currently in place that seem to stumble and trip over themselves at the mere suggestion of a deviation or change of course when the customer wants a change of design or plans. When assembling, constructing, manufacturing, and delivering any product or service, integrated configuration and procedural-based systems can change and reschedule current and future events at a moment's notice, in response to the customer's slightest whim, even when the construction or assembly process is underway, as it simultaneously alerts all those affected of the change, from the largest suppliers to the smallest subcontractor. Add customer control of those systems into the mix and you see that the consumers, suppliers, and manufacturers in today's economy are playing with a whole new set of rules.

Adding to this dynamic of complete customer control, we now have computer-enhanced communication capabilities that can be tied into the project-management systems. Given the capacities of the Internet and the World Wide Web, and how these services can be integrated into electronically formatted messages, e-mail, phone, and fax systems, these configuration-managed and procedural-based systems can readily be made interactive. That's key, because when interactivity is added as a feature in a software system that is integrally tied to the production of a product, there are three remarkable results:

- First, the system (and hence the production of the item or service being purchased) can be monitored by any authorized person from anywhere they have access to a computer and a phone line (the phone line soon won't be a requirement any more).

- Second, an integrated, procedural-based system can *automatically* respond to requests and changes, and incorporate them into the production's scheduled event, while it automatically integrates those changes throughout the system. It then accounts for these changes in *all* future job events in *all* aspects of the system (e.g., design, job costing, scheduling, material orders, accounting, etc.) with minimum human input from the manufacturer, service vendor, materials supplier, or customer. As the system updates itself and reschedules all future events to account for changes (remember the critical-path approach from the last chapter?), it notifies all concerned with the change. For example, if there is a delay or an advance in the schedule, various players in production of the product will get automatic digital messages alerting their systems to the change. Referring again to our example about computer construction, if the customer wants a more powerful modem at the last minute and informs the production line electronically while a computer is being assembled, the system informs all the pertinent aspects of the production line of the upgrade and its systemic consequences. When building a house, if the customers decide they want two extra skylights the day before the roof is framed, the system informs all the subcontractors and material providers of the change and the structural consequences. It then updates the work schedules and even prints out new working drawings that reflect the change.

- Third, a configuration-managed and procedural-based system can be used to streamline the otherwise cumbersome communication among all parties involved in the production and delivery of a product or service. All involved can make decisions based on perfect, complete, and current information about all the aspects of the manufacture, assembly, or delivery of a product or service; all involved get simultaneous access to this shared perfect information because they all have access to the same integrated computer system. These systems "know" what information they need, and they share it automatically.

Now, take a moment to imagine the possibilities of how customers' needs can be met on an individual, customized basis with this kind of interactive, integrated, configuration and procedural-based approach, and how these capacities can dovetail into an e-business future. Some of the brightest organizational experts in the world, especially Don Peppers and Martha Rogers renowned one-to-one marketing systems, have already thought out these implications. (The "Success Stories" aspect of their Web site, www.1to1.com, is a fascinating look at how these business practices have brought dramatic success.) They have given a name to this exciting approach to interactive commerce in this interactive age, a way to deliver highly customized services and products to customers on an individual basis, one at a time, no matter how many customers are involved or what the product is that they are buying. It's called "one-to-one marketing." As it emerges fully-fledged over the coming years, it promises to dominate computer-driven commerce and e-business, as interactive computers rewrite the rules of commerce and of competition.

ONE-TO-ONE EXPLAINED

Let's take a look at how one-to-one marketing works generally, and then see how it can work in any specific industry to greatly affect the service or product provider and, most of all, the customer. The individual customer focus that one-to-one enables is paramount, because with the rising tide of interactive business plans floating about, any business not focused primarily on the individual customer in a one-to-one relationship will suffer at the hands of those who are. As the interactive marketplace takes hold in our economy, it will be focused almost exclusively on a one-to-one basis. Commerce will be built around *your day*, focused and organized around how you do business, individually, not as a category of business, or as a type of business, but how you personally conduct the transactions and information exchanges that make up your day. It's that focused, tied to your *existing* systems, supercharging the efficiency of the existing supply chain, *not* replacing it.

To further understand one-to-one, let's first look at two "givens" of the computer age, features of interactive commerce that are now obvious to even casual observers. The first given is obvious: Computers are able to store, sort, and retrieve vast amounts of information with ease. Secondly, computers and the increasingly sophisticated science of information technology and information management have revolutionized interaction among people and the delivery of timely, current information through digital interactive computer-to-computer exchanges and the World Wide Web. Computers can now talk directly to other computers through electronic handshakes and automatically process information (product specs, billing, delivery data, exchange rates, etc.) that many backward businesses now handle by phone, fax, and mail. For example, if a man is in New Zealand on vacation and he uses his Bank of America ATM card to withdraw money from a New Zealand ATM, he gets New Zealand dollars. But he can go on his personal Web page that instant and see that U.S. dollars have been withdrawn from his account back home. How is this possible? The New Zealand ATM is hooked up to a bank computer that is capable, as most bank computers are, of speaking a universal language of economic transaction. The New Zealand computer "talked" through data maps with his bank's computer in the United States. It used a procedural system tied to up-to-the-instant exchange rates and calculated the U.S. dollar debit amount. All this happened without human intervention... just one computer talking to a series of others through electronic handshakes, procedurally handling a set of complex transactions. This is the kind of communication technology that is now reaching its way through all computer-to-computer exchanges. It is being enabled not just among banks now, but also among industries that may not have had much to do with each other in the past. The technologies making this possible are Internet-based virtual marketplaces and communication hubs that map between unlike systems, or that establish transactional protocols and standards that large numbers of computers can use and share.

It's clear that computers and technology can now make possible monumental changes in the way businesses engage in commerce:

1. They enable a company to *tell customers apart*, no matter how many customers it deals with, and to use profiles of customers to not only service their specific needs but to predict future needs as well.

2. They enable customers to *interact instantly* in a sophisticated, information-rich way with a product or service provider. Computers can now also use transactional platforms and protocols to talk directly to one another, across industries, across platforms, and at any time of day or night.

3. They enable a company to *mass customize* its products and services; that is, to make a custom version of a product or service for each and every customer, and to do so—through the aid of interactive computers—at the same or less cost than it takes to make similar products on an assembly line. (Look back at our examples of Dell Computers and Cisco Systems.)

Let's take a look at these one by one.

TELLING CUSTOMERS APART

Computers have made it easy for a company to tell customers apart from one another and remember them individually, so each can be treated and serviced as if they were the company's *only* customer. Sophisticated Web pages can do this already with ease. Each time a customer uses a Web page for a transaction at, say, Fidelity.com or Amazon.com, the Web page becomes increasingly personal—formatted just for him—as he develops an increasingly robust profile of the services he prefers and the products he purchases. As he uses the Web page more and more, it further refines and remembers what he looks for online. Eventually, the Web page will start to personalize itself for him even though he hasn't directly asked for certain features. In this sense, the computer behind the Web page is starting to predict his needs based on his buying patterns and information requests. A consumer may have initiated his relationship with a e-commerce company by actively asking the Web-based service to assemble lists of products and services. But as he shops and searches over the course of a number of sessions at that site, the Web service learns more and more of his specific interests, and soon enough, it will start searching for (and sending him) information it has looked for on its own. The online service providing this Web page is, in effect, able to tell this customer from others, remember who he is among the millions of users of that service, and predict his individual needs.

More importantly, we are now seeing this kind of service not just with specific Web pages but, by using data-mining tools readily available today, consumers can increasingly have this experience anywhere they shop on the Web. See Figure 3–1.

A company need not have a Web page or engage in e-commerce to take advantage of a computer's ability to track customer patterns and predict needs (though even these kinds of systems typically have their transactions *configured* through Web pages). Let's look at two more examples of single-customer focus, and then finish up with a close look at how business-to-business e-business systems use this approach to recognize single customers.

It won't be long from now when a person can walk to the front desk of a hotel and run a smart card through a scanner that will tell the hotel not only all of their billing information but also their personal preferences: east- or west-facing room; wake-up time; meal preferences; dry cleaning needs, tennis, or golf tee

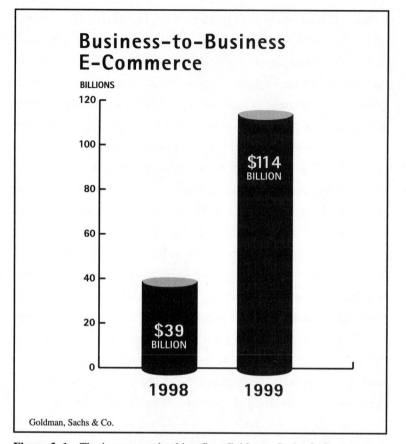

Business-to-Business E-Commerce

BILLIONS

$114 BILLION

$39 BILLION

1998   1999

Goldman, Sachs & Co.

Figure 3–1   The investment banking firm Goldman, Sachs & Co. expects a five-year, $1.5 trillion boom in business-to-business e-commerce in industries ranging from automobiles to medical equipment.

Goldman, Sachs & Co. estimates that businesses generated $39 billion from e-commerce in 1998, and $114 billion in 1999.

times; speed-dial numbers preferences preloaded into the phone; FedEx account number on file, and more. The list goes on and on. There is practically no limit to what a computer can remember. How and where did this information get compiled? The customer supplied it through the patterns he established during his stay at that hotel, at allied hotels, or through requests he made in preparation for his stay. The hotel will obtain and retain this information only after he decides to release it to them.

As consumers customize their buying patterns with particular vendors (hotels, restaurants, clothing companies, etc.), they will return again and again to the vendor that remembers and best accommodates their needs and wishes. This ability to know and remember a customer's preferences—especially when these are tied to that customer's schedule or calendar—can be applied to all types of businesses, from hotels, custom car makers and custom home builders, to landscapers, specialty wine shops, even food stores.

The same technology that assembles customer preferences into a profile can also determine customer pricing on a one-to-one basis. This is already happening now when a person uses his or her buyer's card at grocery stores like Winn Dixie and Grand Union. Those cards identify each customer to a central computer that tracks their preferences. The computer uses each customer's buying habits and grocery volume to determine how to treat and price items for them. For instance, instant coupons may be granted whenever the customer's purchase goes over $100, and even more coupons when it goes over $200. In this way, the price the customer pays for groceries is different than that paid by someone who buys less volume or who buys a different level of quality. This is no different than a "preferred club" rental car status granted on the basis of volume, or buyer's club premiums granted because of allegiance to a certain store. Prices are being adjusted on a one-to-one basis, and computers are powerful enough now to flex and change in response to the buying patterns as they change day by day, even hour by hour.

What's remarkable is that this kind of service and customer attention is nothing new. In fact, computers have once again allowed us to reach back in time to cherry-pick the one-to-one service people enjoyed in previous economic eras. This one-to-one service is a throwback to the kind of service that tradespeople, village shops, and town craftspeople offered a hundred years ago. The difference between times of old and now is that computers have allowed companies of any size to offer this kind of one-to-one service to *any number of people*, from one to one million or more. For those individual customers apprehensive about a loss of control over their personal information, computers have also enabled them to carefully control who gets to know about what they want to buy and when. These privacy features are only getting stronger. Indeed with the sophisticated capabilities of such companies like I2 and Match Logic, consumers are increasingly being given "opt in" rather than "opt out" options, meaning that companies used to assume automatically that you would share your data, and you would have to act to "opt out" of this data sharing. Now, companies are asking first, and you have to "opt in" by declaring your intention to share data. As consumers become more aware of the value of their data, you will soon see that they will demand a share of the revenue it generates, or you will see companies inducing data-sharing participation with consumers by preemptively promising to share those revenues.

Another example of one-to-one marketing? There are plenty. Let's take a look at Amazon.com, the "world's biggest bookstore," which maintains a book-selling Web site. Granted, Amazon.com is e-commerce in its embryonic stage, where the service offers nothing more than static "billboard sales" that aren't truly integrated into other aspects of buyers' lives. But even though the Web site is essentially only a sophisticated document server and Amazon.com nothing more than a centralized book distribution system, they have at least seen some of the potential of interactive commerce. When a person buys a book at Amazon.com, the company not only remembers her billing information (after she sets up her billing profile), it also remembers all the addresses she has ever sent books to, so she doesn't have to reenter her father-in-law's or sister's address when she buys and sends gift books. Also, once a customer purchases a book, Amazon.com instantly compiles a list of similar books other customers (based on amalgamated buying patterns) have purchased, and these are offered at "point of sale."

Not bad for an early attempt at Internet-based, interactive commerce. But it's only the tip of the iceberg when it comes to the capabilities offered through one-to-one marketing. The next step—something that Amazon.com has not mastered, but which is being done by a growing number of e-business companies—is to tie a consumer's preferences and needs to a calendar, set up computers to automatically exchange integrated information about customer accounts, and deliver products "just in time," before the consumer has even asked for them.

Even though the examples of Amazon.com and the smart hotel computer are examples of one-to-one marketing, it is still only e-commerce and not, strictly speaking, *e-business*. The distinction is a crucial one, and a central tenet of this book. E-commerce is where you click and buy from a Web site and static information changes hands in more or less one-time exchanges. This type of buying is often referred to as the "shopping cart" model, where you choose products from an online catalog one at a time, place them in a shopping cart, and check out, purchasing with your credit card. This shopping cart model Web site can remember your profile and buying patterns, but as alluded to earlier, it can't integrate that information into your daily business activities, nor tap into your computer to share information automatically. Why should companies even look at e-business, since the Web is so "hot"? Well, the Web and e-commerce may be popular, but e-business is where the real money is flowing, and e-business sales already dwarf e-commerce sales five to one. Indeed, today's .com e-commerce economy is an extremely immature form of commerce compared to the interactive e-business economy rushing headlong at companies everywhere.

How does e-business come into play with one-to-one marketing and the power computers have to recognize customers on an individual basis? Good question. The answer, simply, is that all e-business is always one to one. All e-business takes to the highest level this principle of serving one customer at a time "exclusively." Here's how: On the most basic level, e-business occurs when your computer talks electronically to another computer (remember our earlier "ATM-electronic handshake" example) to identify products or services that you want to buy or sell. When this happens, you are already in the realm of a one-to-one world, because one computer is talking directly to another, automatically exchanging information specific to one buyer (exchange rates, product specs, preferences, customized features, pricing, shipping information, etc.). These computers can converse across platforms when enabled by a one-to-one company that has established a transactional language that seamlessly maps from system to system (especially seller to buyer), no matter how complicated or idiosyncratic the data. This is one-to-one customer recognition in its most perfect state, because not only is the power of any size company entirely focused on one customer's needs, but those needs can be automatically serviced by tying the computers directly to calendars (to tag products with "need-by" dates), inventory (so ordering and replenishment occur automatically), and the supply chain (so inventory can be managed with real-time data, not "just-in-case" stockpiling). And since we are in a private one-to-one secure environment, payment can be authorized and made in bank-to-bank ("e-cash") transactions. This one-to-one relationship, where the computer can tell customers apart and relate to them as if they are the only clients being served, can save huge amounts of time. For instance, in the world of stock building supplies, for every $25 million spent on building supplies, over 10,000 hours (around five worker years) are wasted handling and rehandling, entering and reentering information, working the phones and fax to track supply, and fixing errors (5000 hours for the builders; 5000 hours for the suppliers). That amounts to around 4 to 8 percent of the overall cost of the product consumed at *each stop* in the supply chain by information processing costs. Many manufacturers, including one major window manufacturer interviewed during research for this book, claim that 20 percent of the cost to the manufacturer can be saved by shipping just-in-time custom products through the existing supply chain. So, clearly, a one-to-one relationship can largely eliminate this waste, by enabling computer-to-computer exchanges of information-rich messages that carry all the information required to buy or sell products, and then track the inventory, delivery, and payment in real time, something that is impossible in non-one-to-one relationships.

Now let's take this one-to-one e-business model and apply it to a notoriously hard-to-control process: house building. First we'll look at a general business-to-business model and then at a highly specific business-to-consumer model.

From the business-to-business perspective, a builder using a one-to-one-capable system can optimize his business by always using an Internet-linked project management system that is "event driven." In an event-driven system, the organization of the job (and therefore all the buying of products and services) is based on a real calendar. Using these systems, anyone with access to the system—customers, builders, subcontractors, vendors, suppliers, and manufacturers—can look ahead and see what specific products and services are going to be needed by when, as each is tagged with a need-by date. Indeed, the need and date can be generated automatically as the computer sorts through the builder's highly detailed schedule and sees, for instance, that all the windows need to be chosen by July 1, delivered by August 12, and installed by August 17. With minimum input or labor from the builder, bid requests, including product specs and quantities, can be sent automatically by computer via the Internet to suppliers, whose computers—which have existing one-to-one relationships with this builder and his computers—automatically shoot back price and availability, as their computers are tied to internal real-time inventory and price updates. But keep in mind that these systems are working with the builder as if he were the only customer "in the store," so to speak: All prices are individual, all services and resources are entirely focused on him. He is not crying out from a crowd of other builders trying to be heard.

Once the builder's computer gets a price, it can automatically accept it (if it's within set tolerances) and automatically place an electronic order that includes date required, delivery location, and billing method. The supplier's computer accepts the order and creates a shipping slip. When delivered, products are checked against electronic records, and signed for, often with a digital pen. With that authorization, the distributor generates an electronic invoice, which is sent computer to computer. The buyer authorizes payment and money changes hands, typically as a paperless electronic transaction. Meanwhile, manufacturers can use this same system to interact with their vendors and suppliers, monitor inventory in real time, see what's selling, adjust production and delivery schedules, distribute their supply based on real-time data (a.k.a. "load-forecasting" or "load balancing"), and stop the costly practice of managing inventory on a just-in-case basis. Why would manufacturers want to get involved in an interactive marketplace? After all, wouldn't they want to link to distributors who could feed them the information they require? There are a number of ways to answer that question, but the main thrust of any response is twofold. First, manufacturers are very eager to get raw data about the buying habits and patterns of people or businesses that buy their products. The processes they now use to feed- and load-balance the supply chain, or to create new products and determine what quantities should be produced, are extremely costly, with relatively high margins of error and waste. Even after spending lots of dollars on mastering the supply chain, many manufacturers still end up "flying blind." So, manufacturers are increasingly eager to use interactive systems to gather valuable raw data about what purchases are being made and where they are being made along the supply chain. Secondly, the value of manufacturers' products is higher if they can brand their product correctly. But to do that they need open channels directly to their consumers, so they can put their product, packaged with their message, directly in front of them. In fact, some manufacturers are even buying distribution channels for this kind of access. But on closer inspection you will find that manufacturers don't necessarily want to get into distribution. (It's not, after all, the easiest business to master.) But it is worth it to them for the data-mining capabilities it offers. The crucial point here is that manufacturers wouldn't have to get into distribution if they were to link to an interactive system. An interactive system that seamlessly linked all the stops in the supply chain could readily be made transparent enough to give them the information they desired, without requiring that manufacturers become part of every aspect of the supply chain that distributes their products.

What has e-business done here? In a one-to-one environment, it has tied a computer's ability to store, sort, and retrieve time-sensitive information and tied it to the existing supply chain to supercharge it with efficiency, single-customer-focused service, and data mining. It hasn't replaced any of the relationships nor centralized the delivery of products (a.k.a. "disintermediation"). It has simply changed how the aspects of the existing system relate to each other, vastly improving their efficiency in the process.

In the next example of a one-to-one e-business, we'll look at the business-to-consumer relationship. When a new house gets built, it must be painted, and a few years later, repainted. With the customer's permission, it doesn't take much for the builder to gather paint-specific information about the consumer (or have the software automatically compile it from lessons learned about the clients from original buying and design decisions). Crucial facts gathered could include the amount the customer is willing to pay for products, her general preferences for quality, what kind and color of paint were used the first time around, the estimated regional service life of the paint, etc.

Tracked by his integrated configuration and proceduralized-based construction project management software program, which is tied to the calendar (the same one used to communicate to suppliers and vendors), the builder is made aware when one of his customers is in need of repainting. With this information (an expressed need) the builder can automatically request that e-mail messages and snail-mail informational packages be sent to a homeowner from various paint companies, containing highly specific, highly targeted information on paint color, price, comparative quality, and warranties for that individual client. The builder can also send the phone numbers and addresses of local paint stores that sell the line of paint that the customer likes to use. The homeowner will likely not consider this junk mail or "spam," because this is customized and precisely targeted information delivered just-in-time, when she needs it. Since the builder knows the house size and paint requirements, he can send the homeowner the information on the quantities and type of paint she will need for siding and walls, trim and doors, and any specialty paints needed to paint unusual surfaces, like masonry. The builder not only ships this information to the homeowner, but, with the homeowner's permission, he ships additional information to area paint stores, so that when Mr. Bates or Mrs. Hancock walks into the store, all their job specs are known, and there's no guesswork on gallon requirements or paint types. After the homeowner buys the paint, the builder can send instructions on how to apply it, if they are applying it themselves, or recommend a painter who has worked well with the builder in the past.

Now, for the builder, much of this is done automatically by his software program, based on the essential job information he collected as he built this client's house years ago. The software enabled the builder to predict the client's needs and fulfill them with little effort. Even better, since this software is tied to a calendar, the builder can follow up with value-added services, even years after first performing work for the client. He can look mighty diligent when he calls the homeowner one year out and offers to come by and do paint touch-up for free, and seven years out when he contacts the homeowner again to see if they would like their house repainted. Chances are the builder is going to keep this happy customer, a customer whom the builder has taken care of with customized service and timely, useful information. And when the homeowner needs painting services at any time, for any part of the house, whether the builder initially worked on it or not, why would the homeowner want to go to another service provider? All her information is already assembled. The homeowner simply contacts the builder, and he simply pulls up the homeowner's file and acts on the preferences that the homeowner provided. It will be in such detail that the builder will know the homeowner's preferences for when the painter may work, how they want their shrubs protected, and even where the painters possibly have to do extra prep around high-moisture areas. I assure you, this one-to-one approach will produce one happy customer and a slew of references. What's remarkable is that the information gathering that enabled this is not the result of costly polling or time-consuming culling of facts from huge data sources. Instead, it happens as a consequence of the ongoing management of any job, or original project specs, by integrated procedural-based project management systems. Do you think your company can benefit from one-to-one service? Though we have used this example for paint, one-to-one service can be applied to the delivery of nearly any service or product, whether it's connected to house construction, the delivery of flowers, the sale of pots and pans, or the purchase of a boat. See Figure 3–2.

This is an example of one-to-one service in an interactive marketplace; it's on the cutting edge of economic change in the Information Age. But keep in mind that there is really nothing new here, just a careful effort made to take supreme care of the customer. When you really look at any one-to-one approach carefully—business-to-customer or business-to-business—you'll see that it takes only the best features of all our past history: the one-on-one personalized service of small village life, the product and material refinements of the Industrial Revolution, and the stor-

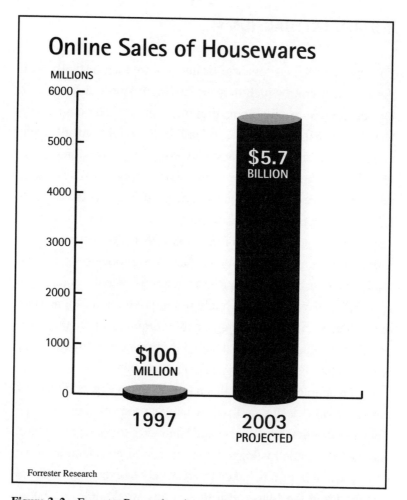

Figure 3–2   Forrester Research estimates that online sales of housewares, including appliances and other home improvement goods, will surge from 1997's $100 million figure to $5.7 billion in 2003.

age, retrieval, refinement, and communication of information by means of computers in the Information Revolution.

Now let's take a look at the second feature of one-to-one marketing and service, instant interaction.

INSTANT INTERACTION

The ability of the customer or business to interact instantly with the company from which they are buying goods and services is the second one-to-one innovation made possible by computers. Customers will soon be able to "talk back" (electronically) and correspond with any company with which they are doing business. These communications need not be simply e-mails or faxes, where the information remains static until it is reentered into a template or computer program. Indeed, these messages can be "smart-messages" that are information-rich and formatted in such a way that the receiving party—typically a computer—can automatically incorporate the data and integrate it into the company's systems, or have it relate directly to the production of a product or service. As customers engage in this communication, they supply highly valuable, highly detailed information about who they are and what they want. Let's take an example.

If a couple that is building a house is also expecting a baby boy, they may designate that the baby's room be painted blue. They work with their designer and contractor to specify the color, and the information is logged into the virtual presentation of the house, which in turn is linked interactively to everyone involved with building the house. But then a few weeks into the house construction, they find out that they are having a girl instead. Now they want to paint the room pink. In the past, this would have presented a real challenge. The parents-to-be would have to call the contractor, who would have to call the painter, who would have to call the paint supply store to tell them the color has changed and not to mix the blue paint but standby for the new color choice. The painter would then have to drop by to pick up new color samples, deliver them to the homeowners, get the new color choice from them, and communicate it to the paint store. Lots of phone calls. Lots of tracking down hard-to-reach people. Yet this is the process so many people building homes are all too familiar with, and when communication channels are crossed this way, too often the wrong paint gets mixed or rooms get painted the wrong color. And that's paint and labor the customer has to pay for whether they want to or not. On the other hand, in an interactive scenario, all of the players who need information about that paint job are linked to interactive systems, which are in turn linked to the critical path of the job. The homeowners find out they are having a girl, and they simply get on their computer, pick the new color from a digital palette, "paint" the virtual bedroom pink with their computer mouse, and click "update." With that, the entire work order, purchase order, accounting system, and procedural system flexes in response to the change. The new color specs are instantly delivered to the contractor, the painter, the paint store, the paint distributor, and the paint manufacturer. Each of their systems imports this information automatically into their inventory, supply-chain management, shipping, and retail management systems, as they also process this data with the data from all the other jobs in that region to balance inventory and forecast consumption based on real need. All this is done without the need for human intervention. No phone calls, no running around looking for the painter, or dashing over to the paint store to pick up new color samples. And all of this happens as a result of the simple click of a mouse at the consumer's computer. (I'll give some other examples of this later in this chapter.)

Let's take another example, but let's really lay out a challenge for the information processing. After all, you may think that a computer is an awful lot of power to wheel in just to change the paint in a baby's room. Fair enough. So with this second example let's take a scenario where the changing job specifications at issue have far-reaching implications. For this example, I am going to use live data: actual dimensions, features, and SKU codes from a real-world company, GE Appliance.

Let's say a homeowner, call him Mr. Andre, is remodeling his kitchen, and he makes a decision on a dishwasher at the design phase of the project, long before the project starts and carpenters' trucks roll up to the site. Mr. Andre went on the GE Appliance Web site and choose a $549 GSD5930DWW, GE Profile Performance Triton Built-In Dishwasher. It has some dazzling features he likes, including triple water filtration and "CleanSensor Technology." It measures 35 inches high, by 23¾ inches deep, by 24 inches wide.

Using a preinteractive system, once the unit is chosen, the general contractor communicates these specs and dimensions (usually by mail or fax) to the designer, who draws up plans. These plans are used to inform the carpenter (for roughing in the framing around the dishwasher), the cabinet maker (for the fine carpentry and countertops), the electrician (for installing power access), the plumber (for locating the drain and feed pipes) and the floor installer (for calculating the height of the floor at the appliance). Each of these subcontractors proceeds assuming the information (35 x 23¾ x 24) is correct. But then a few weeks into the project Mr. Andre takes a hard look at his budget and decides he wants to save a few hundred bucks by buying a less expensive dishwasher. He again looks on the GE Appliance Web site and finds a $399 GSD3910CAA, GE Built-In Dishwasher that he can live with. It's not the top of the line, but it has the features he likes. Great. But there is only one problem: This dishwasher is a different size than the first one. It has the same height and width (35 x 24 inches), but a different depth (25.12 inches). In fact, it is almost 1¼ inches deeper. If it were installed in the space designed for the original dishwasher, it just wouldn't fit.

Using a preinteractive marketplace model, this change would cause enormous headaches for all involved. The carpenter, cabinet maker, electrician, plumber, and floor installer would all have to be sent the new plans, and they would have to rewrite their plans, work stages, and purchase orders to accommodate this change. (Small as it seems, a 1¼ inch difference can have a dramatic effect on plumbing placement, framing, cabinet size, width of countertops, electrical box location, etc.) So, after the new dimensions go out to the subcontractors, the general contractor would have to follow-up by phone, fax, or mail to make sure they will all be working from the newest version of the plans when they begin their work. The appliance order, which must be placed again with GE, must now replace the old order, which has to be canceled. The invoicing and billing has to be recalled and redone, too. In short, this one little change can create a big mess.

Now let's look at this from an interactive scenario, where everyone is seamlessly connected to everyone else. Once a change like this gets made by the homeowner, the new appliance specs, price, and dimensions are sent out electronically by the contractor, integrated throughout the system, and automatically communicated to everyone who is linked to that contractor's interactive project management systems, which are in turn linked to the Andre job's critical path. To make a change of this (or any) magnitude, the homeowner simply gets on his computer, clicks on the new dishwasher he wants, and drags it into the kitchen design. Just as we saw in the above example of the paint changing color, the entire work order, purchase order, accounting system, and procedural system flexes in response to the change. The new dimensions and design specs change instantly. Then these new plans

are integrally upgraded and delivered to the contractors, subcontractors, and appliance supplier. Each of their systems imports
this information automatically into their inventory, supply-chain
management, shipping, and retail management systems. All this
is done without the need for human intervention. Indeed, if the
change is made early enough, before critical path steps were required for the dishwasher's installation, many of the players involved would never even know that a change was made. In its
earliest form, this kind of interaction was (and still is now) done
on the World Wide Web. Large amounts of highly specific information about a customer's preferences and needs can be collected
(if the customer allows it) in ways that are relatively easy to cat-
egorize and sort. E-mail and electronic messaging has also enabled consumers to correspond more often with companies, if for
no other reason than the immediacy of the medium.

As e-business comes into full swing, e-mail will be a sec-
ondary means of communication, because it will require someone to rehandle the information, interpret it, and enter it into a
computer. The more important kinds of instant interactions we
will see will be when one computer talks to another, and anyone
in the supply chain—on a need-to-know basis—is informed of
the transaction and the ramifications of that transaction on their
part in the deal.

Of course, all of this information originating from the customer or the customer's computer won't do a lick of good unless
your company is capable of integrating the information into your
own production system, with a minimum of effort, and—this is
crucial—using it to not only automate the production and/or delivery of a product or service, but integrate it into the individual's
profile in such a way that you can predict their changing future
needs. That way the one-to-one approach allows individual cus-

tomers to say what product they want and how they want it delivered by merely conducting on-going business in an interactive way.

Here's another example: Many appliance manufacturers are now making refrigerators that link directly to local grocery stores through Web pages. When a consumer needs something replenished, he or she simply scans the item at the fridge door, very much as commercial restaurants are able to do now (described in Chapter 2). The grocery store, which consumers used to have to actually visit, now registers the consumer's needs as the consumer's demand data populates the systems that run its inventory and accounting. Scan a milk carton, and milks gets delivered the next time the grocery store sends a delivery (customers can easily control this delivery frequency). Scan a container of strawberries, and strawberries get delivered. As a customer engages the grocery system in this way, they are sharing their data with the entire supply chain so that the milk or strawberry supplier is basing his deliveries on real demand, and he is shipping his inventory just-in-time, rather than just-in-case. As the milk is ordered, the supply chain flexes in response, food gets delivered, and the bank account of the consumer is debited for the products consumed. This is made possible because these systems (consumer's refrigerator, grocery store, delivery van, and bank) have been data-mapped to one another, so that they can engage in seamless cross-platform business-to-business commerce based on real-time demand. Once systems like these come fully online (and functioning prototypes are available now and will soon be on the market), your grocery shopping will be done through these business-to-business transactions. Moreover, as customers use these systems, they will develop more and more robust profiles, so that the grocery can more accurately predict their needs, even down to seasonal fruits, and holiday favorites, and food to avoid because of allergies. This provides a certain "stickiness" to the system, as there are high switching costs to moving to another system: The customer will have to start from scratch building another profile.

Not only will this save your company buckets of money in the production and delivery of your products and services, but it will drive up customer retention (Remember: why would a customer switch vendors when all his information is lodged in one robust profile and the company seems to know his every need before he does?). It will also drive advertising and market research costs down dramatically. Why? The shotgun advertising approach that relies on a single message or slogan—the "one-size-fits-all" approach—is fast going the way of the buggy whip, because now messages can be tailored individually to each and every customer. Customers will no longer sit like motionless targets that companies can inundate with the same message over and over. The advertising message can (and *must*) be tailored to the individual customer's needs, which the company can exactly predict with confidence using interactivity. Even better—since it saves time for everyone, stops wasting ad dollars, and puts an end to annoying junk mail—customers can use the interactive features of e-business computers, automated electronic messages, e-mail and Web-based online services to communicate their instant approval (they buy), disapproval (they buy from someone who better knows their precise needs), or their general opinion of a company's appeal and products.

Is your company or the company you do business with prepared to rise to the challenge of a one-to-one e-business future? If not, customers will switch to one-to-one services being offered down the street or at another Web site. Or they will do their busi-

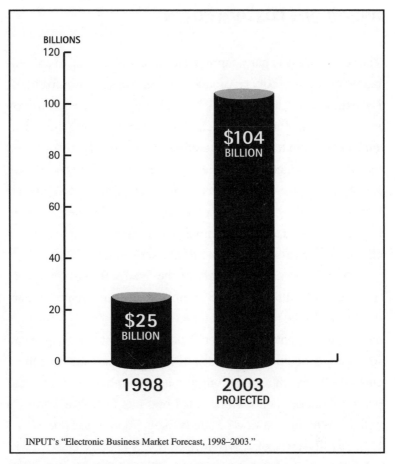

INPUT's "Electronic Business Market Forecast, 1998–2003."

Figure 3–3   The U.S. market for e-business software and services is expected to grow from $25 billion in 1998 to $104 billion in 2000.

ness with a company that can link its computers to the customer's to enable automated exchanges of information-rich messages, respond to the customer's individual needs as they "listen" to them electronically through automated communication, and remember who they are, what they want, and present them with customized products and services in a timely manner just at the time they want or need them.

ONE-TO-ONE CUSTOMIZATION

The ability of a company, through the use of computers, to custom-ize every single product it produces, called "mass customization," is the third principle of one-to-one marketing. Mass customization is not about dealing with special orders that crop up with a con-sumer calling in for an odd alteration or product slightly different than the ones a factory's cookie-cutter production line pumps out. It's about all products being custom. Every single one, whether they are cars, kitchen appliances, computers, tools, even clothing. Here are some small-scale examples that experts point to as mod-els for mass customization in our interactive age.

Note: You need to get rid of the "you." Right now a cus-tomer can go on the Web and compile a custom music compact disc (CD). In the past, if a customer liked a singer or group, they had to buy the entire CD, even if they liked just one song. Then someone came up with the idea of letting consumers compile a custom CD by choosing from among a number of artists, and putting them on their own personal best hits CD. Who came up with it? Who does it now? Sounds like a good thing, doesn't it? Using a fully automated system, a company called CDuctive will ship a customized CD the same day it's ordered. The customer simply goes on the Web site, chooses the songs they want, and a computer burns them into a CD just for them. Mass customization. (The only thing holding back this site is that all artists don't want to participate. Why? They are still living in a world where you were cornered into buying songs you don't want to get the songs you do want. This is a perfect example of the "being controlled" dynamic explained earlier in this book.)

At the Web site for a company called InterActive Custom Clothes, customers can enter their measurements and have a pair of custom-made, one-of-a-kind jeans made and delivered within a few days. The customer chooses the material, color, and fit.

Want mass-customized vitamin supplements? The Web-based Acumin company will help their customers choose a personalized nutritional supplement. They start composing their profile by taking an online diagnostic test. Consumers state their health issues: fatigue, stress, lack of energy. All this information gets rolled into their personal formula, and a unique mix of vitamins, minerals, and anti-oxidants are drawn from a group of nearly 100 components to create tailor-made vitamins just for them.

There are a growing number of these types of companies out there who use technology to customize every single product they sell. This will be increasingly common as computers and software establish more integrated paths to the means of production, whether it's a fabric-cutting machine that can precut fabric to different individual dimensions just as fast as a cookie-cutter fabric cutter can cut fabric all to one size, or a home builder who can let his customers assemble the house of their dreams from scratch at no more cost to them than if they used stock home plans purchased through a catalog.

The examples given are Web-based examples, what is commonly called e-commerce (a distinction made earlier in this chapter). But e-commerce doesn't really even touch the surface of what's possible with one-to-one customization. That's where e-business comes in. Instead of going on the Web and configuring an order by banging in numbers, measurements, and conditions, e-business systems will make that process even easier. What if, instead of compiling CDs, or buying jeans, the customer could manage symbols, drag and drop icons, or manipulate a virtual image of a product and have a computer figure out all the engineering details from there? That's not only possible in e-business systems; it's standard. Or, what if—even better—the customer didn't even have to manipulate symbols or images but simply let their computer talk directly to the computer controlling the means of production to inform it of their product configuration requirements based on other information or other transactions? That's what e-business is all about: allowing computers to communicate through electronic handshakes to spec a product, customize it to the customer's individual needs, and arrange delivery and payment. All with little or no input required from the buyer, vendor, distributor, or manufacturer. All of this is happening on a one-to-one basis, with the entire force of the product production and delivery system focused on a single customer as if there were no other customers dividing its time.

ONE-TO-ONE WINS THEM OVER

One-to-one marketing in this interactive age has changed the expression "If you build it, they will come" slightly: It's now more appropriate to say, "If you build it *just for me*, then I'll keep coming *back*." That's because, with one-to-one marketing, everyone wins. Customers get just what they want, made to order and delivered on time. They also find that—through the Internet—they have a highly efficient means of communicating their wishes to someone willing and eager to hear what they have to say and incorporate it into how they customize current and future products for that client. On the other hand, the company gets to target its product to one customer at a time and deliver it with such a high degree of satisfaction that customer loyalty is a natural consequence of run-of-the-mill transactions. Indeed, the ability of one-to-one marketing to enhance customer loyalty actually *ac-*

celerates with each transaction, because that company's customer profile becomes more and more complete, and the provider is better able to fulfill the customer's expectations *and* predict their needs and desires, thereby further endearing themselves to the customer. Why would a customer switch companies or vendors with satisfaction as high as that offered by one-to-one marketing? This is a crucial point because the Internet has made searching for and switching to competitors simple and painless (a.k.a. "low switching costs"). The bad news for companies not offering a full range of customizable products and e-business communications channels is that the lower the switching costs, the higher the marketing costs. The easier it is for customers to search and switch to companies, the more quickly customers will find companies offering higher levels of service. This means that a company that cannot or does not make itself attractive based on service will have to spend buckets of money to attract new customers and keep existing ones. They will have to do that by using hype and smoke and mirrors to convince customers they are getting a better deal and better service, when they are truly not. Companies that don't have superior customizability, superior one-to-one service, *and* an e-business route to allow integrated, automated communication will end up competing only on the basis of price, something that is already becoming less and less important in the buying decisions of consumers these days.

Another selling point of one-to-one companies is that there is no economic disincentive to offering a full range of services to a customer, whereas with non-one-to-one companies, customers will likely be steered toward only those services that are inexpensive to provide. In the one-to-one system, taking better care of one-to-one customers only gets cheaper. The longer a customer is with a company in a one-to-one relationship, the more profitable that customer is to maintain. This is because the one-to-one company has to invest more to obtain, develop useful profiles of, and educate new customers than it does to maintain existing ones. Plus, as a company learns more about a customer, it can sell that customer a wider range of products and services that are aimed more specifically at his needs. This dynamic is a natural incentive for the company to do the best job it can serving the customer, and it's also a natural incentive for the customer to remain loyal.

In fact, the more individual variations there are in a product, and the more challenging it is for consumers to express their needs in non-one-to-one systems, the more the one-to-one providers will flourish by having the capability to handle customer control and customization—something one-to-one marketing is tailor-made for. And—surprise!—when the customer is treated to one-to-one service, he will be highly likely to stay with that company, refer their services to others, and return to them for more services. After all, during the design and construction, assembly or delivery of a product or service, the producer has compiled lots of data on a particular customer's needs. The customer won't want to start anew with another service vendor, very much the way—from our earlier example of someone walking into a hotel—someone would have to "break in" a new hotel, by building up their profile from scratch. If the service provided were superior, even adequate, who'd want to start from scratch with anyone else?

As any one-to-one relationship grows, the one-to-one company can use the customer information to predict and sell into a wide range of customer needs, whether, to use a house as an example again, it's for regularly scheduled maintenance of the house, warranty renewal, or predictable periodic needs, like landscaping, driveway recoating, gutter cleaning, water filter changing, etc. And if the homeowner needs some service out of the purview of the one-to-one building contractor, like computer maintenance for a home office, or some other professional service like tax accounting or cable TV, the builder can easily provide these by setting up network alliances with other one-to-one companies, thereby establishing a wide network of interrelated service-oriented companies who work with one another in a dynamic and highly profitable way.

When the customer is asked for a recommendation or wants more work done on their own home, like an addition, dormer, or new garage—something in the purview of the builder—guess who they are going to call? Their first call is going to be to the contractor who has taken such good care of all their needs, the contractor who knows intimately what his customers want and how to best provide it in a timely personalized manner. And if they are not able or qualified to do a specific job, they will network to someone who is, and perhaps receive a bounty in the process.

Want to see how one-to-one will flourish in the interactive economy? Want to see how it will spell death to the competition as businesses know it today, and foster unheard-of alliances among companies that used to be the fiercest competitors? Read on and see.

C H A P T E R

Mass Customization: All Products One of a Kind

EXECUTIVE SUMMARY

Computers can easily recognize that any product is essentially a kit of parts and a custom product is merely a reconfiguration of those parts or the substitution of some of them for others. Secondly, a computer can also recognize that the construction or assembly of any product large or small is a step-by-step procedure which can be proceduralized, pegged to a calendar or clock, and tracked (this is called critical-path management). *So, it's really a small technological step to bring the same control and flexibility businesses exert over simple two- or three-step assembly processes, to complicated multifaceted processes, like the building of 10,000-square-foot houses, the construction of furniture, a wardrobe of custom clothes, or the assembly of custom cars from scratch (as we saw in Chapter 2).*

Just as companies are able to use computers to economically customize, control, and change the assembly process for small items, they are now able—through configuration manage-

*ment and proceduralizing of systems—to bring that same economy
to customizing, controlling, and changing the product assembly
at any point in the assembly process, even with complicated processes that were historically too difficult to even track. Add to
this the fact that computers can integrally, interactively tie customers in one-to-one relationships to both the means of production and to all the allied professionals employed in that production process, and it's clear that everything purchased can and
will be customized to some degree. Mass customization. This is
now common with products like computers, cars, even clothing,
and it will soon be the rule for most other products in the new
economy, even the most complicated ones. Moreover, this dynamic
of mass customization will cause a fairly dramatic realignment
of our economy by changing traditional metrics of valuation,
adding value to companies that can accommodate customer control and mass customization, and drawing down the value of companies that cannot.*

*Does control and mass customization like this surprise you?
It shouldn't. It is just the logical result of customer control in the
one-on-one world of the interactive marketplace.*

Mass customization. It seems like a contradiction in terms, doesn't
it? When we think of *mass* anything—mass production, mass
communication, mass media, mass transit—we inevitably think
of the uniform treatment of information and people, or large numbers of identical products pouring off production lines, onto conveyor belts, and into boxes to be shipped to the store shelves and
showroom floors. The notion that a mass-production process could
customize each and every product seems contrary, even impossible. If someone could pull it off, it would be astonishing,
wouldn't it? Well, if you've been watching the digital trade media, and even some popular media, you're well aware that mass
customization is already commonplace in a number of Web-based

businesses, like those cited in Chapter 3. That's just in the e-commerce click-and-buy environment. It will be even more profitable through e-businesses, in their fledgling states now, that can process automated direct computer-to-computer exchanges of highly formatted information. In fact, the every-product-custom e-commerce, business-to-business approach is spreading madly; no business model could be hotter in the view of today's forward-looking analysts. Yet mass customization is no more astonishing to many of the businesses today than mass production was when it first arrived in 1750. Two-hundred-and-fifty years ago, as the Industrial Revolution began to unfold and machines began mass-producing consumer goods, people were used to seeing products made one at a time, each one custom, often constructed by local craftspeople. When machines took over that production, folks were in awe of the fact that a mass-production assembly line could pump out hundreds of identical products. They couldn't believe machines could be made to do such a thing or that the people operating the machines could be so efficient. They were amazed that inventors and mechanics could exercise such precise control over machines, because that was the control they thought was strictly in the domain of the individual worker and craftspeople.

What's astonishing people today is mass-production lines which, through the use of computers, create one *unique* product after the next, at the same speed (and soon at the same or less cost) of mass production. And just as in 1750, what's remarkable is that inventors, mechanics, and computer programmers can exercise such precise control over machines, a control so finely tuned that machines (or the means of production) can reconfigure themselves after each product is produced, not after each thousand- or ten-thousand-item production run.

Consider this a wake-up call, because mass customization will be the model for most economic activity in the interactive marketplace, and companies are doomed to failure if they can't offer customers the ability to customize the products and services they buy *and* provide those products and services at or below the cost of those that are mass-produced. That's true of all products, from shirts and sneakers to houses, cars, and computers. In the coming years, mass customization will in fact become, excuse the expression, *run of the mill.*

MASS CUSTOMIZATION: MASS PRODUCTION WITH A TWIST

The technology and thinking behind the manufacture of one-of-a-kind products at mass-production speeds and costs isn't really that sophisticated. Think about it: What is required to produce or assemble, say, a new computer? It's a step-by-step assembly process, isn't it? Certain predictable steps must precede other predictable steps as the components of the computer are assembled to the customer's specifications. Lots of the assembly process is based on an *if-then* critical path scenario: *If* the customer orders DVD technology, *then* a select number of components have to be installed to enable the computer to feature digital video display. *If* the customer wants a faster CPU, graphic card, and larger hard drive, *then* certain critical paths are followed during assembly. The central intelligence that directs which steps to take originates with the customer and is communicated through electronic messages to the manufacturer's computer that controls production (a seamless computer-to-computer network). That manufacturer's computer, in turn, commands either the production line workers or machines and robots at automated workstations to build that unique product. When the high-tech aspects of a production line are stripped away, the step-by-step assembly of a product today is no different than, say, the step-by-step assembly of a Model T Ford in the early 1900s or a production-loom-woven cloth jacket in 1830. When assembling any product, no matter how high- or low-tech, a certain order of events and steps must be carried out. The car wheels cannot be attached before the axle is installed. The sleeves on a jacket cannot be sewn on until the body has been woven. DVD will not run until the video card has been installed to enable the viewing of motion pictures. So basically, the same step-by-step assembly principles apply then and now, and that will never really change. Each product is really the sum of a kit of parts. The product may change as the parts are assembled in different ways, and the product can be customized if this or that component is added or subtracted on a customer-by-customer basis.

The truly dynamic change in the manufacturing process—the feature that has allowed mass customization in the e-business economy—is the computer's ability to precisely track a practically limitless number of critical paths as a product is assembled. As said in Chapter 2, it is no more difficult for a computer to store, recall, implement, and track a single, limited step-by-step critical path process than it is for it to store, recall, implement, and track a complex multiple-components' critical path, with 1000 or 10,000 steps, even as they change *during* the manufacturing or assembly process due to changes made *while the process is underway*. So, once a computer is introduced to the mass-production process, it enables and equips the producer (as embodied by the various people manning the production line) to remember, keep track of, and execute orders for a practically limitless array of customized configurations and specifications ordered by the customer. The individual workers or workstations don't have to remember everything, just what part they need to play at each step in the product's assembly, though that can now change from product to product. Those specifications are communicated easily enough through electronic messaging. If the production process is highly automated or robotic and the need for human intervention is limited, computers can more easily customize the product, and at a high rate of speed.

Using integrated systems, designers of the production process are no longer limited to, say, setting up the computer-driven machinery to create one identical window, telephone, or stereo system after another. Now the process can be designed so that it can change the product each time it creates one. Each product can be different, as "retooling" can be done instantly and automatically by changing the critical path and components in response to customer demands. Of course, an expert intelligence (either a computer or person) is in the background helping in the construction, maintaining tolerances and limits, and accounting for the design implications of all the changes made to that particular product along any number of critical paths. Impossible? It's not only possible, it's happening right now. Custom computers. Even in a car assembly line. Yes, custom cars. Each one different from the next. A car buyer can visit the new Ford-Oracle WebXchange site and "tune" the car to their personal driving habits and design preferences. The requests are interactively hardwired to the production line, which is interactively hardwired to the supply chain, and that car is made custom. No "spec" products sitting idle on showroom floors. No wasted capital consumed by inventory costs. Another example? At NIKEiD, Nike's Web site, visitors can customize their own running shoes or cross-training footwear. At this site, NIKEiD customers can actually build custom Air Turbulence running shoes or Air Famished cross-trainers. The customer chooses the shoes' base and accent colors, and can even add a personal identification (like a monogram on a shirt) up to eight characters in length. As the customer makes these selections, a rendering of the customized shoe appear on the screen. Turnaround time? Two to three weeks. Price? $80 to $85. As the tools of the interactive marketplace grow more refined and the supply chain is wired and coded to respond just in time to custom demands (as it is at Cisco and Dell, shown in Figures 4–1 and 4–2, respectively) expect one-of-a-kind products at lower cost than mass-produced ones.

From these examples, one can see that computers can now account for the design implications of all the changes made to a product as it is being built. This is a crucial point, because every change made when a product is constructed will have design consequences down the line. Paint a car red, and there must be red bumpers attached later on. Streamline the car's side panels, and standard rear-view mirrors won't work correctly; only a certain type will do. So, any mass-customization process has to have computers capable of accounting for and tracking all the implications of any critical path taken at any time during the manufacturing process, no matter when they are made during the process. And those computers must be capable of not only tracking these changes but instantly communicating them everywhere, dispersing them throughout the system, updating every aspect of the production affected by any change. That's what is meant by the term *integrated*. If, for instance, there is software tracking the building of a house, and the homeowners decide to use the configuration management aspect of their CAD program to redesign the kitchen layout at the last minute, just before the framing carpenters get

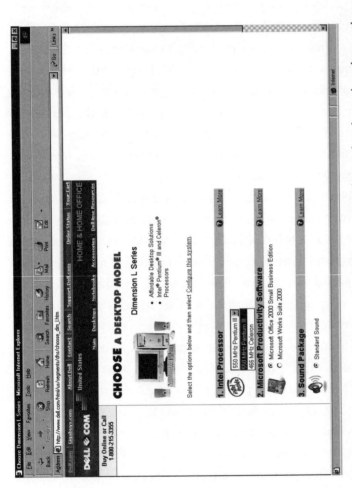

Figures 4-1 and 4-2 Using this web page, shoppers can select Dell computer options and see how prices change when various components are used. This data is hard-wired to Dell's component supply chain, allowing Dell to sell all-custom computers direct, for less than the cost of compatible stock units.

110

File   Edit   View   Favorites   Tools   Help

Back · Forward · Stop   Refresh   Home   Search   Favorites   History   Mail   Print   Edit

Address http://commerce.us.dell.com/dellstore/config.asp?customer_id=04&keycode=6V26&order_code=590408

Go   Links »

Buy Online or Call
1-877-973-3355

Compatibility Messages

General guidelines regarding compatibility with other system options.
Learn More

CUSTOMIZE YOUR DELL® SYSTEM

DELL DIMENSION L

Your Price

Purchase Price   **$889.00**

Business Lease $30 /month (36 mos.)

Update Price   View Cart   Add to Cart

Standard View | All Option View | Print/Fax View

E-VALUE CODE: 6V260 - 590408

Select options, update price and add to your shopping cart below.

Dimension L Series (Required)

The Dell Dimension L Series offers a combination of hardware and services that can grow with your needs while keeping your budget in mind

NEW Dimension® L550r, Pentium® III Processor at 550E MHz
NEW Dimension® L466cx Intel® Celeron™ Processor at 466 MHz [subtract $30]
NEW Dimension® L550r, Pentium® III Processor at 550E MHz
64MB SDRAM

Learn More

Hard Drive

For hard drives, GB means 1 billion bytes; total accessible capacity varies depending on operating environment.

10GB Ultra ATA Hard Drive (7200 RPM)

Learn More

Monitor

15" (13.8" viewable)E550

Learn More

Service

Learn More

Internet

started, the integrated software will incorporate these design changes and account for them in all aspects of the house that are affected. Since the software is integrated, it updates and rewrites the schedule and plans for all future activity (design plans, work schedules, deliveries, and accounting) that are changed or affected by the homeowners' new decision. Integrated systems can do this with any production process or with the delivery of any service, from house building and the making of custom rugs to phone service, travel arrangements, and the design and production of custom cookware, meeting the customer's needs exactly. With integrated systems, the customer can make changes in the design and construction of anything they purchase or consume from anywhere they can get access to a computer or, in some cases (like financial services), a telephone. With wireless Web connections all the rage, soon even phone lines won't be required. Changes of any magnitude can be accommodated by the integrated aspect of the software as it guides the manufacture of products or the delivery of the service at issue. With computers tracking and controlling every step, down to the smallest detail, there is no one to frustrate or exasperate with last-minute changes, no archaic confusing production schedule where multiple managers are making frantic phone calls to change everyone's plans in response to last-minute changes. Instead, consumers can easily watch virtual models of their products being created—all tracked by the integrated software—and they can communicate their wishes virtually, by changing the 3D model (think back to configuration management from Chapter 2, where you simply move a graphic image of your product and the computer configures the steps and components based on the new design). In response to the change in the configuration, computers can in turn send messages—including new plans, material lists, cut lists, whatever—to all appropriate parties. But note that changes made within certain time limits do not slow the process down as they do today, because the integrated software is simultaneously monitoring and updating, on an ongoing basis, all the changes that are made in the product design (think back to our earlier example about the couple changing the color of their baby's room from blue to pink). Computers can then inform and update every aspect of the production system with these changes, as it updates the schedule and billing. Because of this approach—where the software allows the virtual presence of all involved in the process of manufacture, assembly, or the delivery of services—there is a transparent system, where everyone can look in and see where they stand and where the project stands. (This is the feature that defeats the "being controlled" syndrome discussed in Chapter 2.)

Want some more examples? Pontiac-GMC introduced two magazines not long ago, *Pontiac Driving Excitement* and *GMC Directions*. A new magazine, ho hum, right? Only these can be personalized and customized from cover to cover, including coupon inserts, based on the individual reader's vehicle and personal interests. This is possible by cross-matching ownership records with a publishing technology that allows over 20 million possible combinations. Custom publishing. Moreover, this publication has a "learning loop" that allows the magazine to refine the individual publication of each issue, in response to each reader's individually expressed suggestions.

Lands' End's Web site now lets customers view a "model" just their size, so they can try on stock clothes, virtually. (See Figures 4–3, 4–4, and 4–5.) It's not long before that model is linked integrally to the production process, so that the customer's dimensions dictate the actual stitching of the clothes. If Lands' End doesn't do that, do you think another company will? It's only a matter of time.

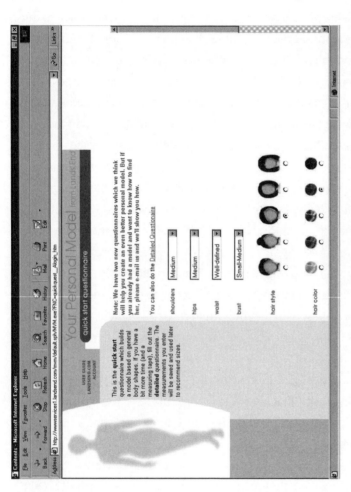

Figures 4-3, 4-4, and 4-5 Using this Lands' End web page, shoppers can create a "personal model" that they can use to shop interactively and build a wardrobe based on their shape and lifestyle.

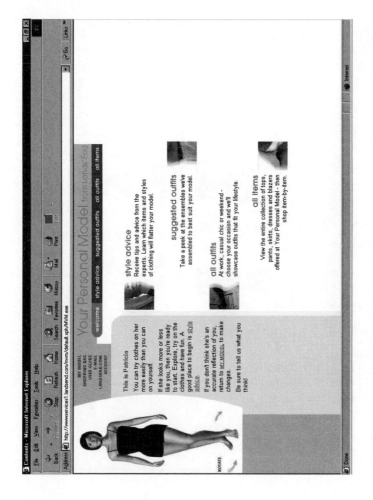

Your Personal Model from Lands' End

welcome   style advice   suggested outfits   all outfits   all items

MY MODEL
SHOPPING BAG
USER GUIDE
E-MAIL
LANDSEND.COM
ACCOUNT

This is Patricia

You can try clothes on her more easily than you can on yourself.

If she looks more or less like you, then you're ready to start. Explore, try on the clothes and have fun. A good place to begin is style advice.

If you don't think she's an accurate reflection of you, return to MY MODEL to make changes.

Be sure to tell us what you think!

ROTATE

style advice
Receive tips and advice from the experts. Learn which items and styles of clothing will flatter your model.

suggested outfits
Take a peek at the ensembles we've assembled to best suit your model.

all outfits
At work, casual chic or weekend - choose your occasion and we'll showcase outfits that fit your lifestyle.

all items
View the entire collection of tops, pants, skirts, dresses and blazers offered at Your Personal Model - then shop item-by-item.

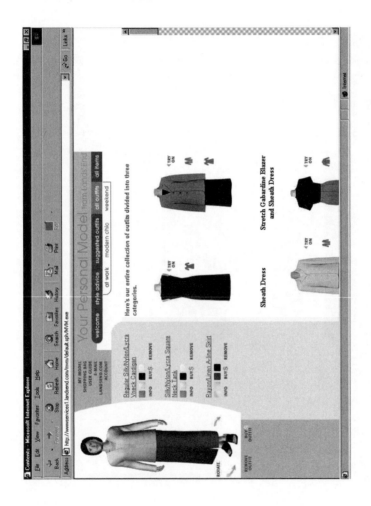

116

Want to customize a commodity? That's possible too. With electrical deregulation underway, power companies are going to have to find ways to personalize the sale of power. They are already doing this on a mass-market basis, like offering "green power" and by distributing "free" energy-saving lightbulbs and reduced-cost, low-consumption appliances. But soon power companies will offer to come to the consumer's home, install PC-based software that could monitor their individual energy consumption, present the consumption patterns graphically, and allow the consumer to customize that consumption, purchasing power at cheaper off-peak rates for high-consumption activities that are not time-dependent, like washing and drying clothes, charging batteries, or pumping water.

"GOING RED": SMART CONFIGURATION MANAGEMENT

Fact: Computers can track (and allow customers to influence) a practically limitless number of work stages as a product is designed and manufactured or assembled. *Fact:* Each step in each of those work stages can be integrally linked to the design plans, work schedules, deliveries, and accounting for any possible configuration and reconfiguration of the product. *Fact:* The design of the products and the control over the production process can be presented in the form of virtual 3D models, like CAD images. Consequently, it doesn't take much to graphically present the consequences (cost, performance, operating expenses, etc.) of design changes so customers can see them *as they are made.* The most obvious indicator would be to have a dialog box on the computer's working screen that reads out instant cost and days-to-complete calculations while the customer is working on the virtual model. Calculations can get even more precise. Why not have the software simultaneously read out other consequential features of the design? For instance, while working with the CAD representation of a house, it will be specifically aware of how much insulation is in each wall, what kinds of windows are in place, and what kind of roof and foundation are used. So, it would be possible to have the CAD drawing not only read out the price and days-to-completion, but also instantly calculate how many units of energy (British thermal units, or BTUs) that house would consume (if the computer knew the average heating degree days for the region where the house is to be built). If the customer were to "drag and drop" the walls of the living room and make them larger, the energy calculator could instantly estimate the number of BTUs the larger room would consume, how much it would cost to build and how long it would take to build it. If the customer were to drag and drop a window upgrade, and an insulation upgrade, the energy calculator could again recalculate the BTUs consumed. This is not only advantageous to the customer in terms of trying to work within a mortgage limit or a yearly operating budget, but it also gives him wide latitude for swapping out products to achieve an optimum balance of efficiency and price; it allows him to fine-tune his home.

For instance, as a customers upgrade their windows, they will find a balance where certain Andersen high-efficiency windows in effect pay for themselves through fuel savings, or an Owens Corning insulation upgrade qualifies them for an energy-efficient mortgage, in effect paying for installing a certain type and R-value of insulation by saving them, say, $20 a month on their fuel bills and $60 a month on their mortgage payments. (This drives home the point that "nothing is a commodity," because even a commodity like insulation can be branded with value-added services like these.) Now, this is a CAD example of a house here, but this configuration management with consequential readouts could be done with any product. Instead of BTU consumption and house design, a company could be using a CAD or virtual model to assemble a car, dragging and dropping the desired features (in effect "tuning" the car to specific driving habits and road demands), mixing and matching features until the maximum car desired matches a price that's budgeted. As the customer is working, the readouts could be for insurance costs, safety feature discounts, gas mileage, likely cost of spare parts replacements based on road performance, etc.

This mixing and matching of features using virtual models with readouts that instantly share the budget and performance consequences of the decisions made is a process called "going red." The principles on which it is based are simple and can be used nearly anywhere. Here's how it works.

With any product, there are only three categorical features that can change when it is designed. In a house design (and most other product designs) only the size (square footage), complexity (building systems), and cost (your budget) of the structure can change. If the computer is instructed which one of these three features not to change, it will give the customer the opportunity to change the other two. When designing the house, if the customer exceeds any of the limits he or she punched into the computer, the screen will "go red" to force him or her to adjust one of the three attributes. For example, let's say Mr. Coyle wants to design a kitchen in his present house. He's got $30,000, and not a penny more. The computer is instructed during the design process that the budget shall not exceed $30,000. So, Mr. Coyle sits at the computer, draws in his present kitchen floorplan, and starts dragging and dropping cabinets, walls, windows, doors, and appliances into place. As he selects from various configurations, the screen will not "go red" until he exceeds his budget. So, he virtually manipulates the CAD design to lay down a Pergo floor, and install Grohe faucets, a GE range, microwave, and refrigerator. The budget calculator is working away, getting nearer and nearer to his $30,000 limit. So, he thinks, why not put in some Vermont red granite countertops? He does, but the screen "goes red." Now he is over budget, and he has to adjust one of the three attribute categories he is working with. Since he knows $30,000 is his limit, and his floorplan won't change, he has to change the building systems or products. He can keep the granite countertops, if he makes a sacrifice in appliances or floor type. So, he simply manipulates the CAD screen, dragging and dropping various items in place, and removing others, using various configurations and reconfigurations until he has the products, design, and price that he wants. When he is done, he pushes a key that tells the computer it is a final design, and the consequences of his design are flushed throughout the design plans, work schedules, deliveries, and accounting systems for the architect, banker, builder, subcontractors, and suppliers.

Another example? Let's say someone has $1500 to buy a new home entertainment center. That customer can visit a site and choose from a variety of items to build that system virtually, with the combined cost of the components reflected in a pop-out box calculator on the computer screen. The site is also careful to steer him to products that work well together, as it prompts him to account for unexpected costs, like connection cables that don't come with the products. He chooses a certain grade of DVD, CD, and tape player, with an FM tuner. Maybe he wants to contract for a DSL line too, so he can download music and video from the

Web. He's still under budget until he gets to the speakers. But then he chooses some high-end speakers, and the system goes red. He's over budget. If he wants to keep the high-end speakers, he will have to compromise on the complexity of the other components. He is in essence fine-tuning his system based on his technical requirements and his budget, with the system keeping tabs on the cost implications of each choice.

This is mass customization at work. Another example? Why shouldn't a person be able to walk into an outdoor equipment store, walk up to a kiosk, and design a tent to his specifications? (Or do it through a Web site?) Drag and drop any of a number of configuration possibilities for material, color, door arrangement, window type, zipper type. Then have the screen calculate the cost and delivery time. Why shouldn't this person be able to walk into a tool store, walk up to a kiosk (or do it through a Web page) and drag and drop tool features to custom configure his own tools, for example, specifying a left-handed tool, a transparent chassis, or cordless capability? Cost and delivery time will be calculated automatically (see Figure 4–6). Once the tool has been specified, it can be linked to all that tool maker's distribution points and sent out with the next load of lumber to that customer's job site, not 4 or 5 days later by UPS to the home address. (Here you see that centralized disintermediation is not the best and most efficient business model out there.)

Now let's take this going-red approach and apply it to an e-business model. As mentioned earlier, behind the configuration-management tools that allow such product design, there is an engineering feature that accounts for all the product specs and design requirements as they change in response to how the configured image changes on screen. Since the product—large or small—is already broken down into its component parts, it's a

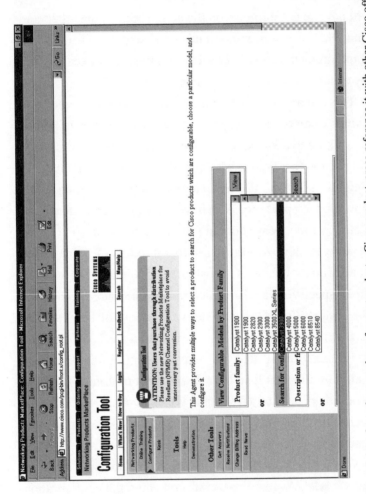

Figure 4-6 Using this web interface, there are lots of ways to select a Cisco product, cross-reference it with other Cisco offerings, and custom-configure them for your system. The configuration engineering is done in the background.

small step to have your computer reach out to the suppliers of each of these component's parts and order them once you or your customer have finalized the product design. The alternative is to have the computer generate a list of the parts in order to call or fax around to find their prices and availability. But why not have a computer do it? Whether it's a house or a computer, why not have the computer use the already digitized information and reach out across an Internet platform to communicate this need to the applicable stations and vendors in the supply chain? The vendors' computers can easily communicate back the price, availability, and installation specs—indeed this can be done automatically. Your business or company's computer can download this information and integrate it back through the system, alerting all the players (outsourcers, subcontractors, bankers, customers), updating the critical path, and rewriting the plans, if it is required. The benefits of configuration management are not limited to the ease of manipulating images by clients. In addition to that, it formats the information in such a way that it can be easily communicated and ready by all the players crucial to its construction or assembly.

All this is possible because the virtual image of the tool, the tent, the house, the car, or whatever the customer designs, is integrally linked to the production of the product. And that integration is possible only because computers can track all the possible critical paths of this kit of parts, large or small, as it is assembled, and link this information out to the Internet.

Does going red sound like some kind of futuristic software that only NASA could develop? It's not. It's not far off at all. Design-build applications, and wide application in the everyday lives of consumers, will be accelerated by wide-bandwidth Internet connections and faster delivery of information, something that even the casual observer of the Information Revolution knows is right around the corner.

WHY MASS CUSTOMIZATION NOW?

How did we get to this point of mass customization? Weren't computers involved years ago in the production of consumer goods as much as they are today? Yes. But computers of old weren't as refined and powerful as today's computers; nor were they integrated interactively into the production process, as they can be today; nor did anyone communicate how consumers could use these tools to make decisions. In the past, computers simply initiated a single set of instructions for the making of hundreds or thousands of identical products, whether they were mittens, computers, cars, telephones, or shoes. And customers who were none the wiser of the possibility of customized products—or who couldn't afford it—simply purchased all these run-of-the-mill, look-alike products without much complaint.

Now computers have really grown up and reached an interactive maturity. This is largely in response to improved software engineering, creative use of computer codes, the falling cost of memory, the availability of universal connectivity through the Internet, and the advent of e-business computer-to-computer communication ability. The result is that sophisticated software and interconnected computers are completely revolutionizing the manufacturing process, making it a configuration-managed and procedurally based environment, highly controllable by anyone who is allowed access, especially the consumer. As stated earlier, computers that drive production can now precisely change each and every product that comes down the production line. But when imagining this, don't limit it only to products on old-fashioned production lines, like tire rims, coffee pots, and radios. Why? Because the principles of mass customization can be as easily applied to traditional products like cars and clothing as they can be applied to individualized, customized products ranging from the exotic to the mundane, from customized medicines, accounting software, food, silverware, and books, to lighting fixtures, soap, televised media, even custom-flavored toothpaste made just for a child by a child. The list is only limited by the consumers' imagination. Each one of these products can now—or will—be customized to individual customer's wishes as they are communicated to the production process through interactive computer links, all integrally linked, often without the need for human managers, often as background exchanges of information from one computer to another.

THE CUSTOMER IS ALWAYS RIGHT... AGAIN

Plainly, improved computer capacity and interconnectivity are the factors driving this new economic wave of mass customization: It has made mass customization possible. But this all wouldn't be happening if it weren't for the fact that customers are demanding products that are customized to their specific personalized needs. For example, industry-leading companies like Dell and Gateway take full and profitable advantage of the ability to customize each and every product, using the principles of mass customization. Every computer they produce is "personalized," custom. They have been very successful with this approach. (Look at their stock over the past two years.) Consumers are flocking to buy these products! Even more importantly, companies like Dell and Gateway have made consumers aware that mass-custom service is possible and at a lower cost than an off-the-shelf product. How? Besides the decreased cost of assembly through the efficiency brought by interconnectivity of computers, there is no inventory carrying costs on unsold products; products are not being sent through the distribution system on a just-in-case basis; a company can control its supply chain of raw materials in and products out on the basis of goods sold, not goods that are thought to sell. Also, because of this overall control, the company holds less bank paper, pays less interest, and processes payments sooner and faster.

With business models out there like Dell and Gateway, increasing numbers of consumers are now looking for the option to customize some of the products they are purchasing. And soon they will be demanding this feature in all their purchases. Old-fashioned companies that sleepily produce run-of-the-mill products that are indistinguishable from one another, or companies that work under the naïve assumption that they can continue to produce noncustom products because the consumers have nowhere else to go, will fall out of favor. These companies will soon be driven out of business by the forward-thinking companies that equip themselves for consumer-controlled, e-business-enabled mass customization. Companies that recognize the inherent rightness of serving the customer's every need will be the ones that survive and flourish.

CUSTOM ISN'T NEWS

How did mass customization seem to come up out of the blue? If it is so clearly the wave of the e-business future, the new paradigm, and the imperative of the interactive marketplace that is gaining such tremendous momentum, then why haven't industries been mass-customizing products all along? Well, in part, mass customization has only been held back and limited by technology. This seemingly recent consumer awareness of customization is only "recent" insofar as the customers are, at last, in a position to do something about their wishes. The fact is, customers have been piping up about their individual wishes for years! But they've been realistic about their expectations. They've long known that custom-made products were an option, but these products were prohibitively expensive because of the time and individual care required for each one's production. It's no secret that, if an individual could afford it, he or she could get custom-made, hand-crafted Italian shoes, a tailored suit sewn in London, or an individually crafted kitchen granite countertop precisely fit to a house's odd angles. In fact, most people want these kinds of quality items, but it is only now with the advent of e-business-enabled computers integrally tied to the production process that quality items will finally be affordable, easy to order, and will not take weeks or months to produce.

Also, besides the technology that is now able to accommodate customized products (see the examples earlier in this chapter and the last chapter) there is an additional dynamic now at work, a crucial feature of the interactive marketplace, and that is the *interactive* aspect that is the focus of this book. Let's define it again: It is the virtual presence of the customer, his money, his personality, and his expressed wishes at a limitless number of places in the economy, communicated seamlessly across platforms and often in an automated fashion from one computer to another. Moreover, the decisions that customers make are not only present elsewhere, but they are dynamic, alive, and can reach out—through deliberate acts or by automated dispersal of information—and affect the creation, delivery of, and payment for products and services. Frankly, interactivity has revolutionized the production of consumer products, not by controlling it (computers did that already) but by welcoming and enabling service providers and manufacturers to instantly act upon the expressed individual desires of any customer buying any single product under construction, assembly, or composition. With *Interactivity*—let's make that a capital *I*—economic exchange and computer technology combine to reach their crowning glory. Interactivity in the age of e-business-capable mass customization is what enables a direct integral link between the consumer and the product he or she will consume. Because of the integration of computers in the production process and the customer's ability to configure products, this link can be accommodated during product design and during the product production, whether it's as simple as a loaf of bread or as complicated as a $1 million house.

To better understand how interactivity works in an interactive economic system, let's take a look at an example. Remember e-mail? It seems like light years ago that e-mail was made possible, yet it is still such a uniquely simple idea that is one of the central tenets around which much of the interactive marketplace is organized.

Many people have become numb to the commonality of e-mail making it difficult to realize what a magical thing it is. E-mail allows a person's intentions to be expressed where they are not present. It allows information that originates only with them to be instantly communicated elsewhere, simultaneously to multiple locations. In this sense, some aspect of a person can be virtually present anywhere e-mail or digital information in any form can be sent (e.g., electronic messaging). But what can we do with this information? Sure, there are lots of social benefits to being able to communicate so effortlessly, but let's just focus on the economic aspects of it. E-mail—messages that have to be read—and electronic messaging of smart data—messages that computers can read allow instant interactivity. And as seen in lots of dynamic Web sites (soon there will be lots more), digital communication allows a person to instantly communicate with a machine, and allows that machine to respond to them and them alone. Impressed? No? Okay, think of it this way. When using the personal Web page a customer has established through the Internet at Fidelity.com, Schwab.com, Amazon.com, or Yahoo.com, the combined mighty power of the company that created these Web pages is laid at his feet. The customer is solely in charge of interactions on the trading floor of the New York Stock Exchange. He commands the undivided attention of that staff at the "world's biggest bookstore." The customer alone has the attention of a search engine that has at its fingertips the resources of 100 million+ Web pages. This is all made possible through electronic messages that actively communicate a customer's intentions and, often as a background feature, economic identity so that he can pay for the products and services he chooses to consume.

What does this have to do with mass customization? Electronic digital messaging is what enables interactivity. When this form of messaging is tied to sophisticated Web pages, which are in turn tied to integrated production lines or integrated service providers—often automated to customize products without the intervention of a human being—then a seamless, fluid, flawless link between the customer's intentions and the products that customer creates, consumes, and pays for is produced. Indeed, any successful business-to-consumer, Internet-based e-commerce must now be launched from an interactive business-to-business platform. Electronic messaging and the virtual presence these messages carry inform integrated sites that are tied to the production of customizable goods and services (delivered in one-to-one marketing arrangements), and these systems are revolutionizing the world of commerce as we have not seen it revolutionized in 250 years, since the beginning of the Industrial Revolution. What's more amazing is that the Information Revolution represents only the beginning phase of the interactive marketplace, and the changes it will bring to this new economy will be equally as dramatic as the changes brought to the world by the Industrial Revolution.

C H A P T E R

Everything Is a Commodity; Nothing Is a Commodity

EXECUTIVE SUMMARY

As the fullest range of prices and products are made transparently available through the Web or through computer access to aspects of the economy that were traditionally closed or proprietary, consumers will see a leveling out of prices among similar classes of products, thus "everything is a commodity." Accordingly, companies in this e-business economy will have to respond in a way that attracts customers to their products, but they won't be able to do it solely on the basis of cutting the price; indeed, the Internet will allow companies to race toward service as the ultimate issue, and when service is added onto a product in a clever way, it will allow companies to charge more than commodity-level prices. So we are now seeing an epic shift in focus among competing companies: As prices level out among similar classes of products and drop away as the primary criteria for whether one product is chosen over another, companies will move to de-commodify their products with value-added services that con-

vince the customer their product is worth having (or even paying a little more for). The company that uses the most creativity and efficiency to deliver one-to-one marketed, individually customized value add-ons to their products will win and retain the most customers, the most referrals, and the most loyalty. This process is called "branding," but branding in the new world of e-business is not just some company slapping a label on a product someone else made so it can charge more for it. In the world of e-business, switching costs are low and, from the customer's point of view, there are no negative consequences to clicking a mouse to find what the competitors are charging, and if it's a better deal, simply moving there. Indeed, it's easy. This has forced companies to brand their products not just with higher service and quality, but with alliances (often among competitors) built into their products that offer customers their own products, services, and competitive pricing as well as relationships to other companies, products, and services (both related and nonrelated). Companies have also been forced to develop platforms that can seamlessly integrate customer information gathered by one company and share it using e-business links to others. That information will be used to bolster overall service performance.

Thus, everything is a commodity *insofar as prices will certainly level out as consumers access transparent systems that compare products across categories. But* nothing is a commodity *if a company is savvy enough to recognize the coming tidal wave of customer control and use the interactive capacities of e-business to identify customer needs and desires, service them on a one-to-one basis with customized products, and link them electronically and informationally to allied companies that can also provide this high level of service.*

It is inevitable that mass customization will become one of the central economic imperatives that drive the interactive marketplace and e-business. It is manifesting (to wild customer acclaim) in many forms now, especially at Web-based custom-product-configuration sites and at companies with e-business capabilities that are run by integrated configuration- and procedural-based project management software. The astute observer of economic and buying trends can't deny that mass customization is an integral part of the future of e-business. Hence, it is easy to spot forward-thinking e-capable businesses now by looking at how readily they embrace mass customization, configuration management, and the automated exchanges of information that make such business practices highly efficient and profitable. Reciprocally, it is also easy to spot backward-thinking companies that are doomed to failure by how tightly they hold onto a producer-control and mass-production, one-size-fits-all mindset, or how slow they are to accept the technological capacity to talk from their computer platforms, business to business, to other businesses on other platforms, so that information can be shared seamlessly.

As discussed in the last chapter, mass customization is especially successful when it is linked to *interactive* integrated procedural-based software that can act on the customer's wishes before and during the manufacturing process and during *and after* the delivery of the product and service. With all this in mind, let's engage in some *n*th-degree thinking. Let's plot out the events currently underway in our economy, look where they are headed, and extrapolate to find the logical conclusion of customer control in the interactive marketplace. If the tools are in place (or will soon be) for consumers to control *some* aspects of manufacture, assembly, and delivery of what they buy, it won't be long before customers are able to control *all* of the aspects of the manufacture, assembly, and delivery of what they buy, for everything they buy. It's really only a matter of time before this happens, given the pace of technology and consumers' increasingly demanding expectations. That's the *n*th degree, the furthest imaginable logical extension of the path businesses are on now: Complete customer control.

The other nth-degree feature of the interactive marketplace is that when this imperative of customer control is linked with the universal connectivity of the Internet that enables cross-platform and cross-company transactional hubs, customers will not stop pushing the limits of the system until they have complete access to all the available products and price points for all categories of product. This is not some futuristic vision. This is happening now, as customers are ruthlessly hunting the Web for just about everything they buy, from computers and watches to furniture and clothing. But complete customer access to *all* products? That's a scary notion to some, but it is an inevitable "disruptive" feature of Internet-based economic exchange: All customers will have unrestricted access to all products, unlimited by middlepeople or companies that have found it profitable in the past to limit access to products (or prices) they didn't want their customers to see.

As the economy becomes transparent in this way, where all the buyers can see simultaneously what all other buyers, suppliers, and dealers are offering *and* charging, prices will tend to reach equal levels among similar types of products. This high-tech dynamic—comparative competition—is just a universal, grand-scale version of tried-and-true economic common sense. It's no different now than 50 or 150 years ago where four grocery stores on the same block competed for business. If all four stores sold essentially the same products, customers sooner or later all ended up buying from the store that charged the least. Or, they bought from the store that offered additional service worth paying a premium for. So, the Internet is not really introducing a new economic dynamic: Customers have always wanted the best services and products. But the Internet is simply making effortless the comparison and acquisition of the fullest range of products and prices, stripping away the obstacles that have traditionally stood in the way of the customer getting what he or she wanted. As the fullest range of prices, products, and services are made available, and consumers see that prices are relatively the same among similar classes of products, the price of the item will become less and less important in the buying decision. Customers will start looking for add-ons, alliance benefits, and service-based reasons to purchase one product over another. As this price leveling occurs, levels of service will rise naturally as a consequence. Why? When a grocery store on one corner starts to feel price pressure from an upstart grocery store down the street, prices will be forced down. But as the stores start to bring distinction to themselves with service add-ons, then prices will rise. (Indeed, among competing stores that add different services to their products to brand them and justify higher costs, they each will be able to charge more than if they were the only store there!) It's been proven again and again in the marketplace that customers won't always buy the cheapest product, but will pay more for products that have higher levels of service, even if they could get the same product cheaper elsewhere.

This is evident in the airline business today. With the advent of the SABRE system (the airline ticket computer system that allows competitors to see the price and times of each other's flights), most consumers know that prices among competing airlines will largely be the same, so they are not concerned principally with the price. Or, if that's not entirely true for all consumers, the price is just one in a list of factors to consider, and it's rarely the first item on that list. What else do consumers think about when choosing among airlines with similar prices? Service, on-time performance, frequent flier miles, ease of access to the terminal, friendliness of the staff, etc. This is a dynamic that will spread throughout the economy as e-business links through the Internet enable SABRE system-type comparison across all industries.

EVERYTHING IS A COMMODITY

As the Internet makes economic exchange, price, and availability transparent, savvy consumers will start to see that much of what they buy is simply products devoid of the glamour a brand name brings. They will see that some name brand items cost more even though they are simply products with a fancy label, and that the label wasn't even attached by the manufacturer, but by the distributor or retailer. They will also see that name brands are often put in place only to hike up the price and not to add any real value, except perhaps the social notoriety and satisfaction one gets from carrying a handbag with a Vuitton label, or wearing a jacket with a Brooks Brothers label even though it is essentially the same product for one-quarter the price. The expression "Oh, I don't want to pay all that money. You're just paying for advertising!" is largely true, especially with regards to camera, stereos, shoes, clothing, or even cars. Generic products—items that are essentially the same as they come off the production line—are branded with a name or are advertised with an appeal that convinces consumers they are worth paying more for.

The fashion industry is a prime example of a sector of the economy that is going to be entirely revamped by a transparent interactive marketplace. Why? Because much of the value of fashionable clothing is in the name brand, not in the quality of the product. Once people start to realize this, they may very well choose to purchase far more inexpensive items that are compositionally identical to similar pricey items that, until now, have been distinguished only by their label. Customers will come to this realization through a transparent system that, increasingly, is already allowing them to view and control the production and purchase of items far, far upstream of the traditional retail setting. And it is giving them the power to actually choose, control, and oversee the raw materials and components used in the creation of what they'll buy, or choose the component aspects of the services they will consume.

What is the net result of the commodification of economic exchange? What will happen when the transparency of the Internet, finally in full bloom, allows consumers to recognize that non-name-brand items are often the same (or have identical parts or comparable components) as name-brand items, but for far less cost? They are going to get the quality they want, but they are going to pay only what it is worth. So, the Internet will not only level the playing field in terms of prices, availability, and consumer control over supply, but it will unmask companies that have been selling less-than-quality items solely on the basis of a name brand, as it elevates products that are of equal quality but cost less.

This transparency—and customers' predictable embracing of systems that enable transparent comparison—will bring about a revolutionary change in the economy as everyone realizes that everything is a commodity. Advertising, hype, celebrity endorsements... so much of what teases out of us the desire to buy, or influences how products are chosen, will be unmasked, as the Internet allows instant comparison of all products, even those not supported by expensive advertising. There will be a shift in the nature of advertising. In the pre-Internet-based opaque economy, advertising de facto appealed to consumers to buy a certain product based on sex appeal, hype, and celebrity—an appeal that tried to persuade consumers to look nowhere else, just to buy. In the transparent interactive marketplace, advertising must de facto admit that customers have vast resources to compare, shop, price, and choose. Ads will no longer try to persuade consumers to make snap decisions based on the appeal. Instead, ads will urge them to make considered decisions based on careful value-judged shopping, shopping made extremely easy with Internet-based programs designed specifically to enable smart consuming. Companies will be forced to compete not with who has the most money for ads, but with who can provide the highest quality, value-added product at the best price with the fastest delivery and highest service. (Advertisements will become less expensive too, not only because of the delivery efficiency, but also because of the ability to highly target the message.)

This is already happening in the computer market. Let's look at the three dynamics at work. First, there are Web sites that are selling PCs at near-wholesale levels. Second, there are companies like Dell and Gateway that are selling custom products at the same price as stock, and third, there are companies like Apple that are selling I-Macs at prices that are dramatically higher than the store across the street or at a nearby Web site. Why haven't people all gone to the wholesale PC Web sites and driven the Dells, Gateways, and Apples out of the market? It's because there has been already a full cycling of the "everything is a commodity, nothing is a commodity" cycle. PCs and Macs were for sale first at rock-bottom prices. But then manufacturing companies used add-ons to raise them above the level of commodity, to assure people they were worth paying more for (e.g., Dell's automated short-turnaround customizability; Gateway's personalized service; and I-Mac graphic performance, uniqueness, and "Think Different" appeal). Twenty years ago if a business school professor were told that there would be three large companies selling essentially the same product for three different prices, he would have predicted they would all fold into one price category, as the three companies fought it out. But Internet access, e-business-enabled companies and shrewd product positioning based on service, have allowed companies charging more to flourish far more than companies selling the cheapest products out there.

Other industries will follow this model. The rise of a transparent economy will make a commodity out of nearly everything that is for sale, because so much of what's on the market today is sold with value (read: *costs!*) added to it solely on the basis of what happens downstream of the actual manufacturing process. The epic shift underway today—for manufacturers, suppliers, retailers, *and* consumers alike—is that consumers will be looking for quality and finding many equitable products available, which they'll be able to compare, price competitively, and verify availability of instantly online. But as prices level out for similar products, customers will also start to look for value *added* to their purchases, but not from some meaningless label, fancy pitch, or celebrity spokesperson. They will be looking for real quality and added service (the Dells, Gateways, and Apples of the world). They will seek the companies that recognize that everything is a commodity until it is *de-commodified* by value-added features that make it worthy of a discerning customers' attention. See Figures 5–1 and 5–2 for an example of how Nike has successfully embraced this mindset.

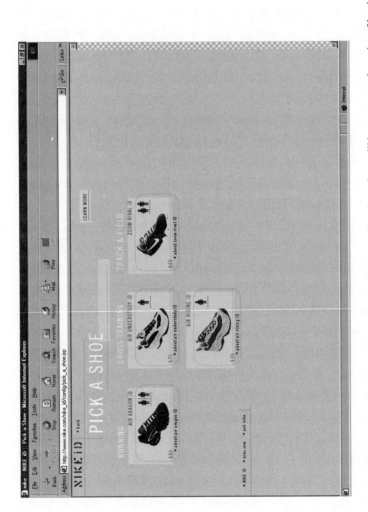

Figures 5–1 and 5–2 Using this Nike web site, consumers can actually design the shoes they will buy, even to the point of having their nicknames stitched into the leather.

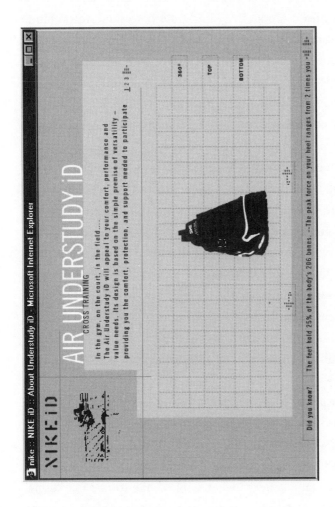

NOTHING IS A COMMODITY

Let's take a non-Internet example of how value-added service *de-commodifies* a product, set in a time before the Information Revolution and the dawn of computers, just to show you how this dynamic works. It's 1950. A man drives into the center of the rural town where he lives, and he needs to buy some gasoline. He knows that all gas is essentially the same product. It's a commodity. In fact, the various stations or franchises that he has to choose from probably buy their gas from the same central refinery. But he has a choice, because the Esso, Texaco, and Mobil stations are all open. Seeing as they sell the same product, he will likely first compare the price. Since the stations are so close together, and they are selling a product that they all paid about the same wholesale price for, the retail price will probably be very competitive, within a penny or so either way. Now, since these stations are selling the same product at the same price—which will be common in a transparent Internet-based economy—they have to find a way *besides price* to lure him into their stations. They have to de-commodify their product by adding value to it. How can they do that?

It doesn't take a Ph.D. in marketing to know that, first, the franchises will have to present their gas stations as clean, attractive places, staffed by friendly people. But the gas station that will win and keep the consumer's business will have employees and policies that engage in what's called one-to-one marketing. They will have to make it a point to know each customer's name and be attentive to their specific needs—remember, this is 1950 and a service station knew how to offer real service. They will know when the oil was changed last, and if the radiator needs to be checked. They will remember that the back right tire leaks and that it may need some air, and maybe they'll even remember that the customer needed wiper blades but was waiting for a sale. If they are really focused on keeping each customer's business, they will have copies of all the warranties on file, and know their buying preferences and how each likes to be billed. With all of this service *offered at the same price* as the next vendor, service-oriented gas stations will have branded their product, and raised it out of the category of pure commodity, because they made keeping each customer their number-one priority. And how do they pay for these extra services if they are selling their commodity gas at the same price as the next guy? With an increased volume brought by more customers in search of good service.

Next—and this is a crucial aspect of how the Internet will be changing commerce—the gas station that wins the customer's allegiance will keep it even if they raise their prices a bit. Why? Because most consumers don't mind paying a little bit more, *if* they are going to get superior service and be treated in a way that makes it clear the vendor values their patronage.

This adding of value to similarly priced products is called branding. Now, the brand "Mobil" or "Exxon" means that the customer can expect a certain level of service and quality, and loyalty… as long as that personalized service continues to be offered, even if these days it's not in the form of personal service as much as it is convenience and ancillary offerings like a deli or bakery.

BRANDING IN THE TWENTY-FIRST CENTURY

Now let's take this branding example out of the 1950s and supercharge it with the capabilities of the Internet and the interactive

marketplace. Remember talking earlier about one-to-one marketing and how it will change the nature of advertising and marketing? The most dynamic consequence of one-to-one marketing is
the interactive computer-enabled ability to identify individual
customers and serve them with the full power, focus, and resources
of an entire company. Does this sound familiar? It's no different
than the 1950s gas station focusing all its personnel and record-
keeping resources on impressing, servicing, and keeping customers. But with the interactive marketplace and powerful computers,
vendors can use the detailed, explicit, robust customer profiles of
a practically limitless number of customers as maps not only for
offering a full array of their own services, but as guides to link to
other vendors in a search for individualized, value-added services
they can repackage or attach to their products, all with the intent
of offering their customers supreme service. They will be using
both the customer's expressed wishes and the expansive informational and service resources of the Internet to provide an unheard-of level of service, presented in the most creative ways
imaginable, on a one-to-one, individually customized basis. The
companies that will truly flourish are the ones that will provide
these services through automated exchanges of information from
the customer's computer to the supplier's computer, or through
the electronic communication made possible by configuration
management (remember our example of going-red configuration
management and the manipulatable CAD drawing of a house).

Won't adding services drive up costs? Won't service costs
spike as profit margins shrink? It may seem counterintuitive, but
shrinking profit margins and rising service costs are *not* necessarily the result of this economic dynamic. With the commodification of nearly *all* products, or, at the very least, consumer
recognition that all products have common commodities as com-

ponents, it would seem that this would drive prices down so far that it would be unprofitable to sell anything but stripped-down generic commodity products, devoid of any of the extras a healthy profit margin used to make available. But there are a number of reasons why this won't be so, as savings and efficiencies will rise with the use of interactivity. First, there is a substantial savings from the super "targetability" of marketing and advertising. As seen in a number of examples in this book—especially based on one-to-one marketing—advertising and marketing costs will be driven down to astonishingly low levels. This will be so because companies won't feel the need to spray their appeal out "shotgun style" to thousands or even millions of people who would never be interested in their products anyway. Further, what outreach is done will be done in a less expensive digital fashion. By today's standards, marketing and sales costs in the interactive marketplace will be a real bargain, offering huge savings, because a large percent of a company's outreach efforts will be focused just on those customers who have demonstrated an interest in the product or service, or have a profile that suggests they might have an interest. For many companies, right there is enough savings for them to welcome the commodification effect of the interactive marketplace. Secondly, discussed in detail in a future chapter, the one-to-one aspect of the interactive economy will yield as much as 35 percent savings just through supply chain management, the elimination of the high costs of retail inventory stockpiling, and the rise of highly focused, customer-specific distribution.

With savings from supply-chain management and reduced marketing and advertising costs—to say nothing of the savings to be found in the reduced cost of market research and old-fashioned customer profiling—companies will be able to heap on the

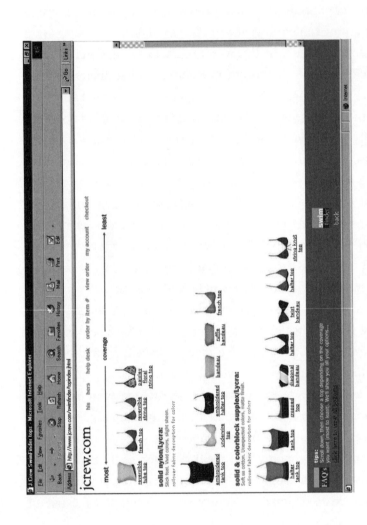

Figures 5-3, 5-4, and 5-5 Choose, mix, and match from among stock J. Crew products, and view the ensemble when you're ready to order. It won't be long before sites like this one allow you to specify the clothing before it is created.

File Edit View Favorites Tools Help

Back   Forward   Stop   Refresh   Home   Search   Favorites   History   Mail   Print   Edit

Address http://www.jcrew.com/swimfinder/bottomindex.html

this   hers   help desk   order by item #   view order   my account   checkout
express checkout

jcrew.com

most ——————— coverage ——————→ least

reversible & tipped nylon/Lycra®:
Two suits in one and contrast color tipping.
rollover fabric description for colors

drawstring skirt   trunk   paisley floral   lowrider bikini   reversible
                                lowrider bikini   string bikini

solid nylon/Lycra:
Slick feel. Vivid colors, slight sheen.
rollover fabric description for colors

wide band   brief   embroidered   bikini
trunk   bikini

drawstring   lowrider
bikini   bikini

solid & colorblock supplex/Lycra:
Soft as cotton. Unexpected colors, matte finish.
rollover fabric description for colors

trunk   brief   stripe   diagonal   stripe   teeny   bikini   string knot
                    back bikini   teeny   back bikini bikini   bikini
                                    bikini

tips:
Scroll down, then choose a bottom, depending on the coverage
FAQ s you want (most to least). We'll show you all your options.
click here to read about...

swim
finder

back

Internet

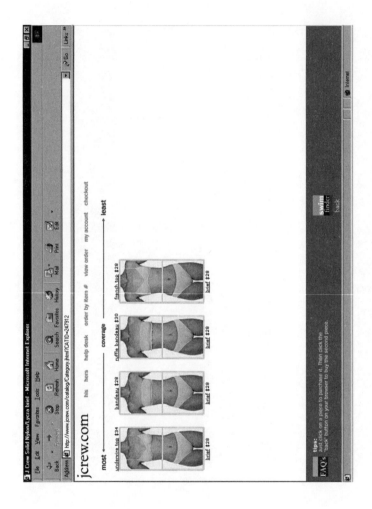

148

services to draw customers and retain their loyalty. But wait. We are not done calculating the savings from the interactive marketplace. Add to these other savings yet another avenue for revenue and healthy profit margins. Companies that provide superior branded service will retain customers at a high rate by generating supreme loyalty. Since long-term customers grow more profitable the longer they remain with the company *and* are exponentially cheaper to retain, they empower the service provider with even more resources to assemble and refine more information and service resources that enhance service for old and new customers alike. A second revenue stream is the wealth of new customers who will be driven to the branded-service company for no other reason than its service (and also for link-throughs to similarly positioned allied companies). After all, won't customers want to purchase products or services from a company that somehow, effortlessly it seems, continually predicts their needs and provides robust personalized service at the same or lower price than the competition?

INTERACTIVE BRANDED SERVICE: AN EXAMPLE

Now let's look at an example of a branded service in order to fully understand how this will work in the interactive marketplace. Let's pick a hard example, one that shows the system at its full power. And again, back to the house-building example, because house building is so complicated a process, it tests the limits of any sales and service system trying to contain it.

Let's say that a company sells fiberglass insulation. Clearly, it is a commodity, because basically, most insulation is made of the same raw material: spun glass. How can this company make its product stand out from all the rest? Well, the company has to brand it. Up until the advent of the interactive marketplace, branding could be done with a special color—pink or yellow—or with a plastic wrapper that made it easier to handle and made the insulation less scratchy. But that's not going to cut it once people start looking through the portals of the transparent economy and seeing that, even with the addition of these incidental and essentially cosmetic features, one product is nearly identical to the other.

The first step toward successful branding is for the insulation company to check its database of customer profiles to see who might be in the market for insulation. They will do this by automatically sorting through the integrated calendar aspects of affiliated construction companies to find the contractors who are just about to go into the buying phase of construction. Or, if the insulation company is branding straight through to the homeowner (so that the customer requests a certain insulation from the contractor), they will look at affiliated bank listings to see which homeowners have recently been approved for remodeling or new home loans. Perhaps the insulation company has a computer system sophisticated enough to be automatically alerted when a building permit has been issued (it is, after all, public domain information).

Once these customers have been identified, the next step for an old-fashioned company would be to snail-mail these prospective customers a flier and follow up with a phone call. But that's not a very dynamic marketing effort, given what can be done with computers. Plus it's very expensive. A company linked to an Internet-enabled, interactive marketplace e-business computer system will be able to do far more. Through an automated system based on a procedural approach that links their systems to the material takeoffs (through CAD images) of the residence in question, they can custom configure an insulation system based on a very specific heat-loss/heat-gain calculation. It will take into account, *on an individual house basis*, the wall thicknesses, door and window types, house orientation, regional heating degree days, and proposed heating and cooling system. Once the ideal insulation package is specified—all with very little human input—the insulation company can show how its product stacks up against all others in online, real-time transparent performance comparison. (Parts of this technology are already in use. Using a going-red scenario, the forward-thinking efforts of Owens Corning have produced a program called Energy FX that lets the customer model a household, swap out components like doors and windows, and compare housewide energy consumption and performance. It's a short step to linking this program integrally to suppliers and lenders.)

To further persuade the customer that their insulation is the best overall value, the company can also propose a number of free ancillary services they will provide with the purchase of their insulation, and if the customer chooses its product, the insulation company can guarantee a delivery date that can be precisely timed so the insulation doesn't have to be stored or left out in the rain before installation. And just to show some customer appreciation, the insulation company can award this customer with "frequent flier" type points they can save up for the purchase of more of their products, discounts at allied companies, or perks, like free travel.

Next, since the insulation company gathered all the information needed for a full-scale energy audit, it can easily provide the customer with answers to questions about energy upgrade payback schedules, heater efficiency, window purchases, and comparative fuel costs. Since the insulation company has precisely calculated how much energy the house will consume, an even greater service would be if it takes that information to an affiliated bank, introduces the customer, advocates for him, and enables him to increase his borrowing power through the savings he'll reap through lower fuel costs. In the end, of course, the real selling point is that the insulation company has provided the customer not with a simple product, but with membership in a consortium designed to serve his every energy and insulation need: heating appliances, building products, bank loan, and more. All this for buying a certain type of insulation. That's branding. That's adding value to a commodity that will persuade a customer to spend more on it, and keep him loyal the next time he is in the market for insulation or any related services recommended by the insulation company. At this point it's clear that by adding value the insulation company has de-commodified its product.

But once the house is financed and built, the one-to-one service doesn't stop. The insulation company can supply the customer with warranty information, survey him for how well the product is performing, and be quick to correct any defects. Also, since the insulation company is maintaining such a close relationship with this customer, it could easily supply him with references for a number of other services he may need, through alliances that the insulation company can easily establish in the interactive marketplace. These could be with the heating and air conditioning companies that can supply yearly service calls and emergency service, or fuel companies who—empowered by the same interactive marketplace and customer alliances—can sell bulk fuel cheaper to these special customers. Will all this necessarily cost more? Initial setup will cost the company something, but since these systems can be proceduralized, the information can change hands with much the same effortless ease and automation as banks exchange information around ATM use. In other words, once the systems are in place and transactional codes written, there is no need for a bank teller or an energy expert processing transactions and information exchanges. They happen as e-business transactions between computers.

Let's take three other good examples. One where a manufacturer brands a product to the consumer; one for a product a contractor may buy for your home (drywall); and one for a product you would buy yourself for your home (shingles).

When all is said and done, "super premium" ice cream is more or less the same product, with predictable levels of quality in its ingredients. But what products stands out among the rest? A company like Ben and Jerry's has a wonderful branding strategy. When you purchase a pint of ice cream, you do more than just hand over your money, you join a family of consumers, and a company with a cause. Ben and Jerry's gives away a percentage of its pretax income to charity, for one thing. They buy products from vendors who treat the environment properly. They treat their employees well. And they put forth an overall look and feel that it is a fun place to work and do business. They have branded a commodity in such a way that paying for it entwines you in an entire philosophy of "business for social responsibility." The ice cream is no longer a commodity; it's a celebration of ideals that you can help promote, and many consumers have voted with their dollars that this is something worth paying a little more for.

Another example: When the homeowner or contractor prepares to purchase drywall, they will see that (like insulation) on close inspection similarly priced products are really identical. But since drywall is a commodity, the interactive marketplace can drive the price to higher levels. What criteria will the buyers use to decide which brand to buy? Let me answer that question with a question: Can you brand drywall? (Of course you can.) That's what the consumer will be looking for. A drywall company could, for instance, offer free installation configurations that enhance its soundproofing abilities and show how its drywall works best in tandem with other products (which they can link you to at a discount). They can even volunteer to take your CAD design and check the framing map to guarantee noise reduction over their competitors' products. They could do the same for moisture reduction, mildew retardation, and painting strategies.

For the roof shingle company, it may choose to elevate itself above the commodity level and justify a higher price of, say, 50 cents more per shingle bundle, by supplying an application video to the contractor, a site visit by a job-site instructor, and e-links to vendors of other roofing materials that enhance the performance of their product (which they can link you to at a discount). They can even provide the installation tolerances that, if followed, would allow them to insure the roof against leaks for 20 years. Worth paying a little more for? You bet.

All this service for the price of ice cream, drywall, and roofing? *Yes.* All this service just for purchasing these products at your fair market price? *Yes.*

So, what are the benefits to these companies? Who do you think their customers will turn to if they ever need these products or related services again? It's no contest, and the cost of serving that repeat customer is pennies on the dollar to establishing a relationship with an entirely new customer. And whom do those customers recommend as insulation suppliers to other potential customers? Again, it's no contest.

Will these commodity items survive as branded-service companies? They will flourish and dominate the market, drawing exponentially more and more customers to them. In fact, these are going to be the only types of companies that survive, the ones that use the resources of the Internet and interactive commerce to supply supremely focused, individualized, customized service at little or no extra cost, coupled with products—even from their competitors—that add value to their own products.

An arsenal of branded interactive e-business strategies could have easily been developed for the provider of any service or product, from makers of custom tea bags and stereo speakers, teddy bears, flags, garden tools, photocopiers, airplanes, and tires, to the providers of banking and accounting services, skin care products, auto detailing, or books. There is no industry in the interactive marketplace that can't take *profitable advantage* of Internet-enabled commerce to economically identify highly prospective customers, deliver services to them on a just-in-time, customized one-to-one basis, and follow through by continuing to offer their own and affiliated services in a way that inspires supreme, continued loyalty.

And what has enabled this service-oriented interactive commerce to flourish? It's the supreme position of the customer's needs as the core of a company's organization and reason for being. And it's the company's selfless recognition that those needs are the sole force guiding the design and delivery of all products they sell.

CHAPTER

Delivering the Whole Product

EXECUTIVE SUMMARY

The efficiencies brought on by the interactive marketplace will force a realignment—not elimination—of the supply chain that will, overall, bring as much as 35 percent savings in some industries. That's because e-business is not only supercharging the supply chain with efficiencies unheard of even ten years ago, but it is changing the very nature of product manufacture and delivery, which in turn is changing the very nature of how products are bundled and presented at the consumer level. Currently the supply chain overstocks warehouses and store shelves by as much as 100 percent, with all the predictable extra costs, just to have on hand what the customer may want at any given time: just-in-time inventory managed on a just-in-case basis. But now supply chain management can take advantage of integrated information resources, company-to-company cross-platform data sharing, customer profiling, and direct integrated tie-ins to the customer's calendar to predict quite precisely what the customer needs when he or she needs it. To do this, companies can use information supplied and harvested in an automated fashion, or that migrates throughout linked systems and populates the computer systems in highly formatted, very smart ways.

As customer needs (represented in digital form) are calendarized and integrated across the platforms of any company serving their needs, allied companies can band together to offer whole-product bundles. These whole products will shine head and shoulders above the piecemeal products and services of old-fashioned companies that don't focus on customer service and that don't take advantage of information-gathering aimed at refining and customizing products and services.

Finally, as whole products are assembled, information sharing will be streamlined, and customer profiles refined (this will happen as a natural consequence of using any interactive system). Consequently, the supply of products and services will become a seamless procedure where even vendors who have never met the customer will be able to predict his or her needs and profit from the one-to-one delivery of the needed product.

In an age where prices will inevitably be similar among similar classes of products and services for each class of buyer, the criteria for choosing (and remaining loyal to) one company over another will soon no longer be a matter of who has the best price. Instead, that choice will be made on the basis of who offers the most welcoming open community for the customer, and how well that community is served by service-intensive, one-to-one focused whole products. Companies that will succeed are the ones that can optimize available information, nimbly integrate it into product and service customization, and deliver to their customers in a timely manner the most finely tuned, individualized product and service available.

The dramatic efficiencies and realignment of product- and service-delivery systems brought by the interactive marketplace offer the opportunity to save as much as 35 percent across the supply chain system in some industries. Impossible? Let's take a close look at exactly what kinds of products and services will be delivered. That's important because the changes e-business is bringing to product and service delivery are affecting the very nature of the products and services themselves. Instead of products and services being sold piecemeal, separately, or as discrete individual items, the packaging and "smart-bundling" of products and services into "whole products" are being offered to communities of consumers brought together by the robust nature of the products themselves. How? These whole-product offerings are not being blindly assembled and presented mass-market shotgun style. Instead, often with the help of automated information harvesting and sharing, each whole product is being assembled as a one-of-a-kind bundle of allied, mutually beneficial, integrally linked products and services delivered just-in-time and customized to the individual customer's needs and desires. (Too abstract? Be patient, examples will follow.) What is so remarkable is that with the arrival of Internet-enabled, mass-customized, whole-product offerings, a truly historic step has been taken in the history of economic exchange. This is what *all* economic activity has aspired to achieve when, a thousand years ago, the first shopkeeper tried to please his customers with high-quality products and careful referrals to other merchants. What is coming to fruition now, because of e-business's ability to integrally link the creation and delivery of custom products and services to customers on an individual basis, is nothing less than the perfection of economic exchange.

Up until now, the economy was largely focused on delivering mass-produced or one-size-fits-all products, and only occasionally would a product vendor or service provider, often for a hefty price, produce custom products and tailored services. Customers participated in this form of economic exchange even though it wasn't exactly right for them because, for the price, there weren't any alternatives. But now things have changed.

Dramatically. Even more dramatic is how quickly our economic system has achieved the ability to deliver these customized, whole-product offerings. Indeed, it has happened after only a short battle with that old mass-market status quo, and the first shots of that battle were fired not long ago when three things began happening:

1. Internet-based companies (or companies that allowed product configuration and ordering through Internet-linked expert systems) began seeing that the Internet generated so much efficiency they could offer custom products for sale at prices that were lower than stock (e.g., Dell, Cisco).

2. Customers interactively responded by showing their willingness to share information about what products and services they would like to buy in the future and, in doing so, saw the advantage of calendarizing their needs so they could be predicted and more easily met.

3. Computer engineers and system architects began creating computer systems that could share information seamlessly, automatically (from back office to back office) throughout entire product creation and delivery systems. Moreover, these systems can now be enabled to engage in information transfers that are directed by the customer's configuration management of a symbol or picture, or even simply because of a calendar event.

It didn't take long for this trend toward the leveling of prices, interactive customer profiling, and community building to snowball, because it was driven with equal fervor from both sides of the economic equation. From the consumer side, customers are eagerly clicking their mouses looking for just-in-time delivery of customized, value-added products, at marketwide price levels, that are linked to allied products with similar value and customizability. (Remember from previous chapters: When switching costs are so low, product delivery systems and prices are presented in transparent systems, and there are no negative consequences for a customer to shop around, customers will gravitate toward service- and value-added communities despite record marketing dollars spent by competitors that simply offer low price.) From the product and service providers' side, forward-thinking companies have been fiercely competing to find and refine the efficiencies and business systems to offer these whole products and prices. But for the providers, this is coupled with a need to know more precisely who their customers are so they can fine-tune those products and systems, and offer an even greater range of products and services in mutually beneficial, value-added arrangements with allied companies that can be linked through the Internet.

Now these trends have become *the* paradigms of the interactive marketplace: Prices are leveling out and the result is that as they level out, price will soon no longer be the principal basis on which customers purchase one product instead of another (the auto industry is a prime example of this, where many people know they can get a car for less, but pay more for service add-ons). Instead, customers will be seeking the most individual-customer-focused community to be part of, the one that most thoroughly takes care of their daily needs. That is so central to the changing nature of the economy and to the central themes of this book. Once companies come up to speed with the efficiencies offered by the Internet, prices for similar classes and categories of products and services—even customized ones—will be so similar among competitors that customers will only cursorily consider price when choosing to buy one product over another. That's largely due to the changing nature of *how* products are delivered and the efficiencies found in the e-business economy. But interestingly it's a dramatic reversal of one of the most widely accepted and basic tenets on which all economic exchange is based. After all, it's always been true that the merchant who sells his or her product for the cheapest price gets the business, right? Not any more. Price will become less important over time as the paramount feature driving a buyer's decision.

If price will soon no longer be the basis for choosing among similar products, then the nature of the product itself has to change in some way to attract consumers. Indeed, the product itself will have to be materially supplemented or packaged with value-added services and innovative delivery methods in a way that will convince customers that the product in question is a greater value than a product from a similarly priced competitor. And how can that whole product be best assembled? Companies are using the full gamut of software and informational resources to tailor and integrally link products or services to one another. They are then taking those whole-product offerings and linking them integrally to the customers' daily lives, whether they are individuals or businesses, so the product or service delivery becomes automated (as does the harvesting of important information before, during, *and after* the sales event takes place).

How will customers respond to these types of offerings and how will they choose among competing companies? Well, it won't take long for customers to recognize which personalized, customized, value-added products and community of fellow consumers suits them best. They will also soon recognize which companies are trying to limit their choices by entrapping them in confining cul-de-sacs (e.g., limited choice, limited selection, nontransparent pricing), and which companies are consistently doing the best job assembling attractive whole-product packages that put the individual customer's needs first. Once companies bring distinction to themselves as particularly able to serve the customer, and deliver the best value-added products time and time again, they will find a community assembling around their company and its allied partners. That community will, in essence, present the customer with "higher switching costs," but the costs will be imposed on the consumer by the consumer, as a natural consequence of good service. In short, they like what they see, and they won't want to click their mouse or switch companies for a number of reasons, including: *a*) They like how services are targeted just on them, how all the resources of a literal army of allied companies are all working for their individual benefit; *b*) They won't want to start from scratch with another company to build up the robust profiling information necessary to maintain a successful one-to-one relationship; *c*) Their experiences to date have generated a high comfort level, and they will have fond memories of people they met through their purchases or of community-enhancing experiences they enjoyed while shopping. (Think of how much more rich an experience it is to shop at Barnes and Noble than to shop at Amazon.com. Even though both offer online access, Barnes and Noble has a wonderful, friendly store atmosphere for the whole family, and, because of this community-building feature, is winning the battle with Amazon.com.)

Once companies have won over customers and convinced them that they legitimately offer superior service, they can raise prices for their products. Customers by and large will remain loyal because their relationships to a provider company and its allied partners are based not on advertising, hype, or false promises. They are based on superior branded service, customization, individually configured add-ons, innovative just-in-time delivery, and unrestricted free choice. Companies that will shine are the ones that can optimize available information, nimbly integrate it to product and service customization, and deliver to their customers in a timely manner the most finely tuned, individualized product available.

Does this sound crazy? People spending more for a product they can easily get for less elsewhere, especially when switching among competitors is so effortless? It's not crazy. Indeed, it's human nature. Some daring companies have taken profitable advantage of it for years, even before the e-business parade rolled into town with its brass band blaring. An example of this has been provided in Chapter 8 with a brief look at Hertz, a company that has managed—because of supreme customer service, loyalty program add-ons, and discount relationships to allied vendors—to charge above-average rental car prices in a tight commodity-price-driven market. (That philosophy will put them light-years ahead in the interactive marketplace, because they've already learned the hard lessons that e-business will teach a raft of other companies.)

Keep in mind that when we see the leveling of prices in this interactive marketplace, as prices seek their own levels among similar classes of products for each person, this will happen not just with products offered online through the Internet. This leveling will be broad-based and flushed throughout the entire economy. (Remember the example of grocery stores competing in a small town? Well, extrapolate that out through other sectors of the economy.) That's partially because so much of our supply chain and retail systems are ripe for being optimized by the informational resources of the Internet. But it's also true because of the way competition will be more open and pure. It will be carried on in transparent environments, as the engines of commerce, supercharged by the information revolution's resources, push *down* production costs and the costs of the traditionally wasteful supply chain, as they push *up* everyone's ability to forecast demand (which, as we get closer to absolute forecasting, will go the farthest toward truly leveling prices). This dynamic will allow costs—no matter where products are sold, online or at your corner grocery—to seek a more uniform competitive level.

WHO WILL SUCCEED?

Who will succeed in this e-business realignment? It will be the companies that can deliver both savings and value-added services as they cleverly employ all their resources to create and deliver a package of goods and services that make up the most desirable, individually focused, integrally delivered, customer-service-driven whole product. The enduringly successful companies in the interactive marketplace will be the ones that are agile enough to recombine and reconfigure these packages quickly (or in an automated fashion) in response to customer whims, or the latest greatest product offering combination. They will do this only if they can respond to changing consumer tastes and are watchful enough to deliver products or services that are not just isolated items that consumers anonymously take away without integral contact with the provider companies. Instead, companies must act as agents that bring a wide range of product and service offerings, and these products and services must come with a full complement of anything directly or tangentially related to them that make them the most robust customer-focused, customer-satisfaction-driven items imaginable. Moreover, these sales must be interactively, integrally linked to the consumer through configuration-managed, procedural-based systems tied to the individual customer's calendar of needs.

Failure will come—slowly at first, but surely—to companies that equate low cost with value or that fail to see that low cost is always just a fad. Failure will come to the companies that offer anything less than the whole product or whose profits depend purely on selling high volumes of stripped-down products delivered by stripped-down means. Failure will come to companies that try to monopolize customers and *direct* them to a limited array of products, rather than *attract* them with an expansive array of specific goods and services, whether they sell them or whether they help consumers to find them for sale elsewhere (yes, even if that means giving up the sale to a competitor). The successful companies, on the other hand, will be the ones that best accomplish the goal of supreme customer service and fulfillment. Success will be a matter of one-to-one service, and the company that can call upon the full range of Internet-enabled features and e-business computer-to-computer solutions to provide that full range of products and services will succeed. That success will come with the product or service provider ever mindful of how easy it will be for consumers to switch among competitors. It's already not even as hard as walking across the street to another store; it's already as easy as a click of the mouse.

To put all of this theory in motion, let's take a look at a couple of examples. The first example is a look at the bundling of products and services from an imaginary alliance of co-opetition-based companies. The second is an example in today's marketplace, as this theory is applied to show how whole-product companies like Barnes and Noble will flourish because they are a "clicks and bricks" company that combines the best of the Internet's immediacy with the best of community-based traditional retail. Competing companies that rely solely on commodity-level prices, like Amazon.com, will falter, unless they take on this whole-product mentality. Many people may wrinkle their brows in disbelief at this claim that the Amazon.coms of the world will fail unless they ally themselves with customer-service-focused products, but the facts bear this out. It doesn't take a Harvard MBA to see what Amazon.com must do. Indeed, it could be as simple as buying a bookstore chain, decentralizing its shipping, and making book purchases more timely and convenient (something Wal-Mart is aiming to do with its online model). But they must do, essentially, what Barnes and Noble has a big head start on: combine all available resources to provide supreme customer service and make buying a community experience. The resources they could call upon include the latest Internet search engines and individual profiling, alliances with premium vendors (as seen with Barnes and Noble and Starbucks), attractive, comfortable, inviting locations, and products available locally the day they are ordered over the Web. If Amazon.com can't move as fast toward Barnes and Noble as Barnes and Noble is moving toward Amazon.com, its days are numbered. Keep in mind that Amazon.com already spends disproportionately more marketing dollars per book sold than traditional bricks-and-mortar bookstores. Indeed, between 1997 and 1998, Amazon.com more than tripled its marketing dollars from $11.5 million to $37.5 million to maintain its growth, and newspaper articles that pointed out increased sales also commonly contained such language as,

"Swelling marketing costs pushed Amazon.com deeper into the red..." (*Seattle Times*, October 29, 1998). In 1998, a year when Barnes and Noble and Amazon.com were clearly competing head to head, Barnes and Noble's annual revenues topped $3 billion, and its net income rose 73.7 percent to $92.4 million (a bottom line that will only be helped increasingly by Web sales), while for the same period Amazon.com's revenue was $610 million with a *net loss* of $124.5 million.

Why the loss and the need for more and more marketing dollars? There are two primary reasons. First, for consumers the switching costs among online vendors are extremely low. At Amazon.com, it's as easy as clicking a mouse to switch to another Web site to see if, say, BarnesandNoble.com or Buy.com has a better price for the same product. Indeed, there are few negative consequences to going elsewhere to buy books. Second, soaring marketing dollars are required if all a company is offering is low price. In part, those marketing dollars are spent trying to *remind* (some call it pestering) customers that they are paying more elsewhere, while trying to *distract* them from the added value they may be getting elsewhere in terms of robust customer service, instant availability, or a sense of consumer community. If the Amazon.coms of the world are to survive, they must leave behind the disintermediation model and their dependence on discount prices. Instead, they have to take a whole-products approach that keeps consumers at their sites, or, perhaps, expand into retail locations where the buying experience is supercharged by Internet capabilities and the community experience is enhanced by an enticing ambiance and the presence of allied vendors. This essentially makes switching costs higher, and the consequence to the consumer of switching to another vendor would be the loss of the value-added ancillary services.

ASSEMBLING THE WHOLE PRODUCT

Let's take the various aspects of the interactive marketplace that have been introduced throughout this book and assemble them into one mighty engine of commerce. Let's take all the aspects of Internet-enabled, calendarized, configuration- and procedural-based management systems, and combine them with imaginative vendors who want to use these systems to provide one-to-one marketing in the mass customization of products. Further, let's look closely at this through a product-delivery system that brands products with superior service tracked by integrated software linked to affiliated products and services. So let's assemble the pieces.

For most people in both the business and personal realms, there are an essentially limited number of products that are needed to predictably run our lives and businesses smoothly. And since these things are needed predictably—whether it's a gallon of fresh milk, 3000 gallons of heating oil, 100 bundles of roof shingles, or three bags of grass seed—they can be delivered precisely, to the day and often to the hour, they are needed. (If someone can't predict or remember when they'll need certain products replenished—who knows when it's time to put in a new furnace filter, for instance—then software customized by the manufacturer can help predict service lives, consumption schedules, duty cycles, etc.) Let's further refine this concept of the products needed to run our lives, because whether a person runs a business or a household, most people are not just looking for any gallon of milk, but for a specific kind of milk; e.g., locally harvested, organic, 2% milk. For the 3000 gallons of heating oil, domestically produced #2 oil is preferred, and only 500 gallons at a time in six deliveries, all on Monday mornings after 7 A.M., every two months. For the 100 bundles of roof shingles, sand-colored, fiberglass, 30-year shingles are desired with the warranty registered automatically; delivery should be timed to 6:30 A.M. on the morning after the roofing contractor finishes tearing off and cleaning up the old roof. (This date can change due to weather, so the software planning the delivery better be able to track job progress, day by day.) Packaged with those shingles, the manufacturer-recommended roofing felt, 24-gauge flashing color-matched to the shingles, and hot-dipped galvanized nails are also requested, along with installation instructions for how to overlap the shingles for the specific hip roof that the roofers will be working on that day. For the bags of grass seed, zone-5, frost-tolerant, Kentucky bluegrass, with one bag for shady areas and two for sunny areas is preferred. It should be accompanied by a rented seeder, and the correct number of bags of fertilizer customized to the PH of our local soil. The local college kid job pool is notified by e-mail that there's a day's work at a certain address waiting for anyone who wants to make a few bucks. (They'll be able to respond easily to confirm they are available, and lock in a contract online.)

You get the picture. No one wants one-size-fits-all products or services. They want the products customized to their specific needs, and they want the delivery timed in such a way that the products are there just when they want them, no sooner and no later, with allied local services contacted automatically.

Now, from the demand side, there are two essential components required by e-business and the interactive marketplace for the timely delivery of customized service. First, the customer has highly specific needs, and second, this customer has a calendar (or clock) that tells him or her when these needs have to be met or fulfilled. Knowing these two pieces of information, a company can build a computer-based, Internet-enabled, interactive e-business product-delivery service that can easily plan ahead enough to get products to the consumer via the best path, whether that is overnighting them, shipping them by truck, delivering them electronically, or even having the consumer pick them up at the local grocery store.

For this to be done, there has to be a technology acceptance level among the consumers, because the software that will track these needs and arrange delivery—to customers of all sizes, from large businesses to single consumers—will have to be fully integrated into the daily workings of the person's life or business. And no matter what kind of product is delivered—some will actually go stock, not custom, because that's how customers want them—it will be packaged into a whole-product offering. This will happen because the different steps in the supply chain won't be eliminated, but supercharged to modify, prepackage, and preassemble products for individual consumers. The supply hubs that used to focus on mass numbers of customers will now be able to focus on individual customers, bringing to bear the full resources of their company on that customer as if they were the sole focus of the entire company. This is one of the central tenets of the one-to-one marketing approach from Chapter 3. (Keep in mind here that technology is used to *enhance* the design, configuration, and delivery of existing products.) Customers interactively will be able to log on, get information about their products and enter information about how they want them specifically configured. Indeed, as these individual customer profiles become more robust and are shared among vendors, the system can easily become so sophisticated it will tell the consumer when they are about to purchase the wrong product. (For example, if a customer tries to buy a spare part for a Sears washer, the computer may have in its records that this customer owns a GE washer; when a cus-

tomer buys compression faucet parts when their faucets are ceramic disk-type, the system can advise them of the proper choice.
This kind of cross-referencing can happen seamlessly and automatically across the range of manufacturers, vendors, suppliers,
and even be integrated to the cash register at the local home center or grocery store.)

As this system monitors transactions and shares information
in a common standardized platform with other participating vendors and suppliers, it never eliminates the retail setting, nor eliminates any aspect of the supply chain. It just optimizes them. It just
enhances them. Products that used to be delivered piecemeal for
the customer to assemble (*just think* how many stops are required
or items that must be purchased individually to, say, put an addition on a house or wire a basement) will now come customized,
preassembled, prepackaged, and preconfigured. There still will be
a retail setting for impulse buys, pure shopping, and purchases of
things needed that day. But for many items, the need for having
something right away will be largely eliminated by ample supplies
of products shipped by branded service suppliers and vendors who,
with lots of lead time, have worked with consumers or used their
profiles to predict needs, and offered the goods and services to be
delivered so they'll be there when consumers need them. (It's this
kind of load forecasting that will be a major factor in leveling
prices, because there won't be a visible disparity between prices
of bulk sales and "convenience" points of sale. The price will level
out somewhere in the middle.)

Moreover, consumers won't feel the need to dash off to the
high-priced store to get something of which they've run short.
Why? Because the integrated system can easily arrange to have
them there ahead of time, based on replenishment cycles it will

learn from the consumer's buying patterns. But what's more, these proceduralized systems that deliver goods and services—based on predicted need, needs expressed by electronic messages from computers, needs expressed by profiles, or needs measured empirically by job-management systems that track a job's progress and can "see" exactly what is needed—will work just as well for someone running a household as they will for a housing developer building 15,000 homes a year. With enough foreknowledge of the need and the time it is required, astute forward-looking companies can enable their computer systems to supply any good and any service in a timely way, with most of the information required for that sale exchanged automatically among the participating companies' computers.

It's wrong to think that this kind of system will work only when the business owner or consumer spends endless amounts of time at the computer punching in numbers and product codes. Indeed, after initial configuration, the processing costs will be at an absolute minimum. That's because the system is built to internalize and integrate this information as it works with consumers as they live, shop, and work. It learns incrementally, discovering patterns, assimilating tiny fragments of information, and collecting them from any product or service vendor who shares the common interactive platform. It learns the customer's habits and consumption cycles, composing an ever refined identity for each consumer, integrating the information seamlessly into the system's intelligence. And it only gets better and more refined with use, as, with each transaction, it corrects for errors, oversupply, poor timing, or miscalculations in quantity or labor, and accounts for these errors when it recalculates the delivery of the product or service the next time.

SUPPLY-SIDE WANTS AND NEEDS

Are systems available now that can accommodate, in a timely fashion, so many individual wishes from so many individual consumers and deliver them with better efficiency than the current retail system? Can the supply chain be so dramatically enhanced? Yes and yes. This can and will be done through integrated one-to-one computer-driven systems. It's happening now on a small scale, using consumer-to-business e-business models from the Web and business-to-business e-business models like Cisco Systems. It will be happening on an increasingly larger scale over the coming years, as customers and companies realize the benefits and savings.

Here's how: When a consumer becomes Internet-enabled through a computer, or a business links itself up to the Internet, they are effectively linking themselves to a world of interactive commerce. This is especially true if they use e-business-enabled systems that link to hubs that have established cross-industry or cross-platform transactional communication standards. By using such integrally linked systems, e-business-enabled companies are taking the giant steps toward electronic supply chain management and absolute load forecasting, where dramatic savings can be found by allowing the seamless flow of information to replace the labor-intensive manual handling of information currently contained in phone messages, faxes, and mail. These e-business-capable companies are availing themselves not only of these efficiencies, but they also enable their companies to compose whole-product offerings that efficiently (often automatically) bundle products and services that would otherwise be delivered piecemeal by companies working separately, rather than through cooperatively sharing resources, discovering synergies, and sharing referrals. By using "smart casting" and the absolute load forecasting described above, they can predict consumption cycles precisely. By doing this, they enable further savings by managing fewer items in the supply chain (no more just-in-time inventory managed on a just-in-case basis).

Further savings can be found when procedural-based calendarized computer systems are integrated both in the consumers' lives and businesses, and in turn integrated into the myriad services providers set up to respond to automated demands with mass-customized products, all assembled with the service to the customer as the paramount goal. Let's take a look at just such integration.

THE INTEGRATED INTERACTIVE MARKETPLACE IN ACTION

Let's say a man runs a small software company—or, analogously, any business, manufacturing, or service concern. In the past, once a month, let's also say his office manager went to the store or ordered by phone 60 reams of photocopy paper. Up until the advent of the interactive marketplace, that purchase was a static purchase, and the ability to extrapolate other needs of his company based on the purchase of 60 reams of paper was virtually impossible. The office supply store simply sent the paper along on its truck, happy for that sale.

But wait. With the integrated marketing capacity of the interactive marketplace, that purchase of 60 reams of paper is the key to unlock (and profit from) other service needs of that company, and the companies that will prosper in the interactive marketplace are the ones that group together (actively or automatically through preestablished pattern linking) to gang their branded ser-

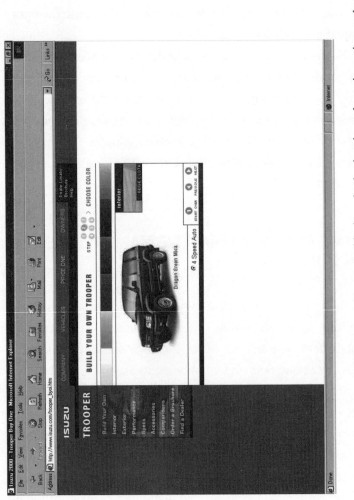

Figure 6–1 Through a six-step process, you can build your own Trooper at this site, selecting interior and exterior options and colors. A real-time calculator adds up the cululative costs of each choice.

vices together into whole-product offerings. After all, if a company consumes 60 reams of paper, an individual can guess their size and predict other needs, based at least in part on the need profiles of other similarly sized companies, which can easily be ganged regionally and examined for consumption trends. Interactive companies that share common platforms and information sharing can take advantage of this information and offer this customer not only reams of paper but all the attendant services required of a company that size. Let's look closer at this example, because this same approach can be used to predict the needs of nearly any individual consumer or company, and it shows how the interactive marketplace will work in an integrated fashion.

For the company that supplies the 60 reams of copier paper, if they were astute and eager enough, they would recognize this paper-buying pattern and offer to deliver the paper automatically, on a regular schedule. After all, if on the 15th of every month for the past five months the office manager has called and asked for the paper delivery, it's a pretty safe bet the office manager will call again next month and the month after that. So, the supplier can offer to simply take over this product delivery tracking (oversupply and undersupply can be adjusted based on precisely predicted needs). It's a nice service to offer. It shows how they value the business, and it relieves the office manager of that task. The supplier can offer an easy-access personalized Web page for when the office manager wants to change the order or adjust the delivery amount.

But there is even more service opportunity here—offered not only by the Interactive marketplace, but also by the one-to-one relationship enabled by the reconfiguration of the traditional supply chain. The paper supplier can also guess that a company that consumes paper at this rate will also need copier repair and cleaning services at a predictable rate too, right? So, on that personal Web page, offered just as a service to keep the consumer coming back for more paper, the paper vendor can offer a link to an allied copier service center, and because of that alliance, offer the service at a discount; just click on the desired make and model. The office manager will appreciate it if he can click on a Web page, check the paper order and with another click of the mouse, have a copier service technician at the door in three hours.

Since the company consumes paper and copier repair services, they must consume other office-related material as well: printer cartridges, disks, computer hardware and software upgrades, postal services, shipping, office cleaning, furniture, printing, graphic design, copy writing, management consulting, etc. So, as far as the paper vendor is concerned, why not offer—as a whole-product service offered to retain that paper business—links to other service providers? Why not offer these services through alliances set up so that discounts can be passed along to this customer? It can all be done interactively through a personalized Web page, at little cost. And the new vendors won't have to spend time assembling a customer profile, because it will be shared in the cross-platform language that these companies use. The customer enters pertinent information just once, with permission to share it, and the system integrates it among vendors. (This is why companies will be able to predict the needs of customers they have not even met. But keep in mind that the customer decides if he will participate, not the vendor.)

This approach benefits not only the customer, who has one-stop shopping at a Web-based interactive vendor who seems to have predicted their needs, but it has benefits for the vendor too, as it has a higher profit margin working with companies and consumers who use these low-cost ordering systems, and a payment system linked directly to their back offices. Even better, a system like this has a very high customer retention rate, because advertising and marketing costs are kept to a minimum (after all, a vendor's branded service is its own best advertising). Yet stops have not been eliminated along the supply chain. There are still suppliers, retailers, wholesalers, and manufacturers. It's just that they've been supercharged with integrated information that allows for carrying far less inventory while still having enough on hand to cover the full range of customer needs. And, indeed, by bundling products and services to be delivered from single rather than multiple delivery sites, they see even more savings, some of which they can pass on to the customer as discounts that keep them coming back for more, and some of which they can take as profit.

Now let's take this notion of integration another step and not just maximize the supply chain's efficiency, but automate its operation. This can be done by pushing the actual action required by the consumer or vendor entirely into the background. That's what calendarized, configuration- and procedural-based integrated job-management software does. It tracks the progress of daily patterns for a consumer or business in real time and detects their needs. Then it reaches out to all concerned parties to alert them to what is required and what other products and services might be needed, so they can be offered at opportune times.

Let's take the house-construction business. Much of what goes into the building of a house—lumber, fixtures, tile, pipe, paints—is presented in traditional retail settings, and much of the cost of a house is wrapped up in paying for the waste generated by that supply chain. But what if there were systems that knew every step that had to take place for the building of a house, systems that knew every specific product that was required? Then it wouldn't take long for a software program to generate specific needs, couple them with the dates and times by which those needs must be fulfilled, and tell the supplier how some of these products can be preassembled or prepackaged for the builder's specific needs on a day-by-day basis. By knowing when products, preassembled product packages, or product bundles are needed, the integrated system could simply count back the days it needs to assure timely delivery, whether it's two days for a box of nails, or two months for custom tile or windows. The software can pick up these dates during the preplanning of the project, as soon as the CAD or design configuration of the house is finalized.

Remember earlier in this chapter, the two features we needed to know from the demand side to design a successful interactive marketplace system were a *need* and a *time* by which to fulfill it. Well, if there is an integrated system that is aware of the specific needs of a business, the time or date of the required delivery, and the steps that have to be taken to install a product or consume a service, then it wouldn't be all that difficult—given the awesome power of computers—to design a computer tracking system that communicated directly with a factory or supplier to have products assembled, custom configured, and shipped directly to a building site. All of this moving in a steady stream of staged deliveries that provided the products, accompanied by any added informational material required for their use.

Since this software tracking system would be calendarized, keyed to days and even hours of the day, and could flex and respond to changes in the calendar as entered by the workers in response to job site delays or schedule advances, it would be able to take over much of the ordering and oversee timely delivery of these goods. All this would just be a residual consequence of the job-management software. It could look to see, for instance, that on August 12th, the roofing will start, and since it knows that it takes sixteen business days to get the roofing to the distributor and two more days to get it on site (information the local distributor can use to avoid having too much roofing on hand, dramatically reducing his costs), the software can send an electronic purchase order that is automatically integrated into the local distributor's delivery system. The software would also automatically order all the other materials required for the installation of the product: nails, roofing felt, flashing, etc., based on past requirements for similar jobs. And, perhaps through the "alliance building" engaged in by the roofing supplier, the computer could also offer to the job site managers affiliated services that are required for roofing: scaffold and ladder rental, insurance, warranty tracking, gutters, and roof vents, or even labor pools.

And how will all these goods be paid for? Well, it won't be the traditional 30-, 60-, 90-, or 120-day "float"—that costly and frustrating system of 30+-day net pay used by everyone along the supply chain. Instead, payment can be easily arranged directly, through electronic transfers that can be carefully tracked by the same computer system that's so closely tracking the job's progress and ordering. The results from this efficient timely transfer of money alone will be huge savings that can be passed on to the consumer and taken as profit. Couple these savings with the savings and efficiencies generated by both one-to-one alliance building and integrated management of the supply chain, and you'll find still more savings, which can also be taken as profit and passed on to the consumer. This can only build more loyalty.

Remember the prediction made earlier: The dramatic efficiencies and realignment of product- and service-delivery systems brought on by the interactive marketplace offer the opportunity to save as much as 35 percent across the supply chain system. Where will we find those savings? Let's see by means of an example. Earlier in this book we looked at "configuration management," where a consumer simply manipulates an image and, in the background, the real information processing gets done. If, say, the consumers are building a house and they decide, after designing their bedroom, that they want to add night tables to either side of their king-size bed, they are going to want the room wider. So, they configure the bedroom image and use a mouse to drag and drop the walls, making them wider. As they make this change, its consequences are instantly reflected in the critical path required to build the room the new way, and those affected by the change (suppliers and builders) are instantly alerted through integral links from the room image to their computer systems. This goes on in the background, of course, and many players won't even know that the room size was ever changed. They see just a list of bedroom specs when the critical-path management system prompts them to do their assigned tasks. In preinteractive marketplace days, before configuration management was possible, the supply chain had to handle this change in bedroom size manually, and the architect/designer, and suppliers of lumber, insulation, siding, roofing, and windows, along with the builder, subcontractors, and the accountants for all involved, would have to stop the building process, check the design change, reappraise the materials order, recalculate the material and labor costs, and forward this information on down the supply chain by phone, fax, and mail. The costs associated with this are enormous, perhaps 5 percent or more *for each stop* along the supply chain.

Some companies, notably Wal-Mart, have installed supply-chain management solutions that alert the supply chain as soon as a product is sold off the shelves. (Wal-Mart's supply chain is integrally linked to in-store cash registers nationwide.) But with the interactive marketplace, and integrally linked configuration-managed systems, there is now the opportunity to link the demand to the supply chain even before a purchase is made, not after a product is sold. When the bedroom specs are finalized and products are ordered (all based on a configured image) the interactive supply chain flexes in response, automatically alerting the computers that monitor and control each link. The implications of this in terms of work saved are monumental. But think too of the money saved if this approach could be used to forecast real demand and stop the supply chain from blindly supplying products on a just-in-case basis. The money saved here too is substantial, to say nothing of what can be saved by integrating a payment system to the supplier, banker, contractor, and customer and shrink billing cycles from today's 80 days to under 10, or even down to 0.

Upon hearing this scenario, the 35 percent savings figure may be considered *low*. But also note that those savings were not found by eliminating any step in the supply chain. There are no layoffs required. Indeed, the supply chain will just work more efficiently, with little waste, optimum exchanges of money, with customer service as its central organizing principle.

THE WHOLE PRODUCT VERSUS THE PARTIAL PRODUCT

There is a huge battle going on these days on the Internet between Barnes and Noble and Amazon.com. Rivers of ink have been spilled on predicting which company will succeed. One is a brick-and-mortar approach married to an online presence (Barnes and Noble). The other is simply an online presence (Amazon.com).

Yet for all the commentary, it really doesn't take much to predict which one will survive. It's clearly Barnes and Noble, and it's for a number of very simple reasons. They are better equipped to offer whole-product offerings; they have stores that are a pleasure to visit and that act as a supplement to their online presence, and most importantly they have used the Internet technology to enhance an existing service rather than to create a service from scratch using only a technology as the basis for the business. Indeed, if Barnes and Noble had been an early-adopter "clicks and bricks" company and used the Internet-based fulfillment system that now powers Amazon.com, there would never have been an Amazon.com. Let's take a closer look, using this Barnes and Noble/Amazon.com battle as a metaphor for e-business, keeping in mind that there are lots of other such battles underway, and crucial lessons to be learned in the comparison.

Companies like Amazon.com that depend on the Internet as the sole purveyor of their products offer no tangible community aspect to their sales; they offer no value-added whole products, and they have mistaken low cost for value. After they roll out their offering of low prices, they have little left in their arsenal to supplement their product once someone else comes along selling books for the same price with the same clever Web-based customer profiling. One of the maxims of the interactive marketplace is that prices will level out and companies will compete not on the basis of price, but on the basis of the service and the community they generate. It follows that companies like Amazon.com, which get their identity solely from delivering low prices and disintermediation, will be beaten in the marketplace by companies that, for the same or nearly the same price, can offer service-added products in pleasant bricks-and-mortar locations that combine the benefits of bricks-and-mortar stores with the advantages of disintermediation—low price, unlimited selection, fast delivery, easy database/inventory search engines, smart profiling. This is especially true in an age of switching-cost differentials as dramatic as the ones we see in the comparison of Barnes and Noble and Amazon.com, now that Barnes and Noble has become a "clicks and bricks" store, with an online resource and lots of comfortable retail locations. Essentially, Barnes and Noble has generated an allegiance and community because of their value-added whole-product offerings. As a result, it costs less money for Barnes and Noble to retain customers. Because the switching costs incurred by the customer are high (loss of access to whole products), customer retention is also very high. On the other hand, switching costs for customers of Amazon.com are very, very low, and the resulting marketing costs very high. Amazon's marketing costs will only rise instead of fall, as they try to retain repeat customers. That's because there is nothing but low price to hold them at Amazon.com's site. So, to continue doing business, Amazon.com has to lure new customers, or through marketing, advertising, and outright hype, convince repeat customers what a deal they are getting, even though a couple clicks of the mouse will disprove that claim. Customers will find they don't pay any price—no higher costs, no loss of service—by going to another online book-selling service. On the other hand, if the customer has developed a relationship with the Barnes and Noble whole product, there is a real price to pay for switching booksellers. Here's why: When a customer goes to a Barnes and Noble store with his family, he can already walk up to a kiosk, put in his name, and find the system telling him if Barnes and Noble carries the books he is interested in. Soon, these systems will be linked to the Web and the point-of-sale system, and a profile compiled from his past purchases (made in-store and online) will allow the system to tell him about other books he might be interested in. It won't be long before, as he is standing there, the computer will alert him to the fact that a puppet show is starting in five minutes in the children's book section. That's where his son will go, as his wife heads to the interior design section with her list of suggested books, and he heads off to look at business books. Through this kiosk, they've ordered drinks from the in-store Starbucks, a latte for his wife, a grape soda for his son, and a Coke for himself (something the system will log in for their next visit). As they gather in the food area later to enjoy their drinks, they browse the covers of books they haven't yet seen or heard about. Later at home, he realizes that there is a book he saw that he really wants to buy, so he goes online and orders it from home to be delivered overnight. While he's at the Barnes and Noble site, he sees that his profile has been updated from his most recent purchases with some interesting books added to the list. All this for the price of a book? Yes. All this for the price of a book that's essentially the same price level, if not the very same price, as the book found on Amazon.com's site? Yes. Now guess which company this customer will show his allegiance to?

Amazon.com is trying to make a "disintermediation play." They have tried to find their savings (and all of their profit) by cutting out steps in the supply chain rather than by using informational resources to enhance the supply chain to improve customer service. (They also forget to factor in the leveling of book prices that the Internet will bring about everywhere in the book supply chain, in stores *and* online.) The cost of this disintermediation play, of course, is personalized customer service. If you have one company that offers e-business-enabled, personalized customer service, comfortable stores, online or store-based sales, and the opportunity to make shopping a social event, pitted against a stripped-down product delivery system that offers products at the same price as the whole-product location, it's clear which one of these will succeed in the long run. And when a customer decides to go on the Internet to order a book, they will more than likely click on BarnesandNoble.com, because that company's identity is still fresh in their mind from their last pleasant visit, and frankly, they know how to serve many of their customers' needs in a personalized way.

While the example above focuses on Barnes and Noble versus Amazon.com, the same comparison can be made for any other whole-product vendor that combines an online presence with bricks-and-mortar stores like Gap and LL Bean and pit them against vendors simply trying to make disintermediation plays, like Peapod.com or Toolsonline.com. In a world of leveling of prices, one-to-one service, and mass customization—the successful companies are the ones that take full advantage of informational, integrated resources to service the customer as they reach out to allied companies to maximize that customer service. These are the companies that will shine, flourish, and profit.

Now let's read on to the next chapter to see how this dynamic whole-product approach will mean death to competition as it exists today.

C H A P T E R

The Death of Competition as We Know It

EXECUTIVE SUMMARY

Interactive one-to-one commerce will become the dominant mode of all future economic exchange—businesses are unstoppably heading there now. But a unique business dynamic is also emerging, enabled by both the ability of one-to-one commerce to automate information exchange and the transactional standards that these exchanges require. Companies are starting to see the benefit of sharing data and standards—even among competitors in "co-opetition" alliances. Soon, the competitive edge that old-style companies used to gain by monopolizing an industry sector will give way to full-fledged co-opetition. *Co-opetition is an increasingly popular business strategy, written about recently by Adam M. Brandenburger and Barry J. Nalebuff, where companies embrace their competitors if the skill- and service-sets offered by the resulting alliance enhance customer service. How? Using one-to-one focused services that share integrated data through open platforms, a customer can engage in business with any single cooperative alliance member and find all other alliance members—whether they have met the customer or not—able to pre-*

189

dict their needs and offer superior, attentive, individualized, branded service from the very first moment a relationship is established.

Using these alliances, co-opetition companies will be able to create a critical mass of customers that will enable low-cost, high-profit commerce with a shared-asset, procedural-based, one-to-one approach. This will not only generate an astonishing rate of customer return, but it will give allied companies the ability to predict demand, focus their marketing and sales efforts on a single-customer basis, and load-balance inventory with a much broader market view than they would have if they'd worked alone. Companies working together will generate far more efficiency, sales, and loyalty once they realize that co-opetition arrangements have a far greater chance of succeeding if they focus solely on serving the customers' needs and stop treating customers as captive pawns willing to be monopolized. These days, with switching costs so low, very few customers will stand still and watch companies limit service and choices only to boost corporate profits. They will switch quickly and effortlessly to another service or product.

Competition as it is today will die away, as the new one-to-one interactive economy punishes companies that build walls or that don't offer customers integrated products and services as a standard aspect of any sale. The type of competition that will grow and blossom in the interactive marketplace will be cooperative systems that allow companies to thrive only at what they do best and most efficiently. Organizations shrewd enough to be early adopters of open-format cooperative competition and one-to-one marketing will add vastly to their customer bases through the customer-service-enhancing features of this approach and the fierce loyalty it generates.

Competition in today's economy is ruthless. Dog eat dog; win at all costs. In advertisements, it's depicted as a battle or war, a storm, a fierce duel. The best business minds in the world have taught that it's good when one company rolls out all its guns to go against another company or group of companies, driving prices down and service and quality up. It's the same in the world of international commerce too, per the mantra: "Open markets and let competition rule!" This is the accepted wisdom of capitalism and it is heretical to suggest it works any other way, or that it should be in any way changed. But this book takes a contrary, even heretical view of competition. Why? The emergence of some fiercely competing companies, on close inspection, do far better to cooperate than compete. Oddly, this cooperation works to the vast benefit of the companies and the customers they serve. This realignment of traditional competitors is brought on by the interactive marketplace and low switching costs, as e-business and a transparent economy deliver the death blow to competition as it is today and usher in synergistic relationships called co-opetition. To make this all clear, here are some examples.

Years ago, when the first ATMs emerged, Citibank of New York decided that they would set up their own proprietary ATM system. There were few ATMs in existence anywhere at the time, so Citibank figured they'd corner the market by making ATMs that would work just for people who held accounts at Citibank. Citibank thought that if they gained an early monopoly on ATMs, they would draw people who wanted ATM convenience to their banking system. Did it work? No. It was an utter failure. Here's why: Other banks recognized their customers would soon demand the convenience of ATMs, but they saw that the best ATM system would allow customers to use as many ATMs as possible, in as many locations as possible, even if that meant losing control of a few customers who would, now and then, use ATMs maintained by competing banks. So, these banks—normally fierce competitors—banded together to create a common, shared, open transactional format for ATM transactions that any bank could use. As they built their joint ATM system, it was not focused on trying to exclude other banks and greedily monopolize customers. Instead, the guiding force behind the system's design was focused solely on the customer's convenience; it was a system that put customers first. So, when a customer from, say, Chase Manhattan Bank wanted to use an ATM, they'd be able to plug their card into any ATM, whether it was from NationsBanc, Chemical, any bank at all... *except* the ones from Citibank. Citibank held on to its proprietary ATMs, until its own customers started to realize they'd have far more choices and far more convenience if they opened their accounts at banks that offered a wider choice of ATMs, instead of the narrow choice offered by Citibank. It wasn't long before Citibank saw the error of its ways and joined the multibank ATM system. As a result, they retained those customers who were thinking of switching, but probably lost an even greater number who resented Citibank's attempts to monopolize their business. Had Citibank taken the lead in the open-format ATM systems, and let customer service focus and guide the development of their system, who knows what kind of loyalty they might have generated. They didn't see soon enough that if a business practice is not in the best interests of the customer, it would eventually lead to a loss of market share.

Did all the banks benefit in the end? Sure they did. First, the fees they charged at the ATMs weren't limited to just their customers; indeed, they had a larger customer pool to draw from than if they'd limited their ATMs to just their customers. But secondly, each bank—through its efficient ATM, superior service, and convenient locations—could present its services to a wide variety of prospective customers. If those services proved superior, customers would switch banks, at an extremely low cost to the bank that gained the customer, far less than if they'd advertised and fought for that customer on the open market.

This is a prime example of where the interactive marketplace is headed. The ATM example is co-opetition at work. A group of traditional competitors sees the perils of trying to monopolize limited numbers of customers and instead bands together to share information that simultaneously expands all of their business opportunities, as it consequently builds strong customer loyalty and reduces the cost of doing business at the same time. How often does a sales rep get to offer a complete product that will reduce costs as it increases customer service and market share? In the interactive marketplace that uses e-business-enabled communication tools, this will be the norm.

Cooperative arrangements like these have a far greater chance of succeeding if they focus first and foremost on serving the customers' needs and not treating customers as captive pawns willing to be monopolized. These days, very few customers will stand still and watch service and choices limited in service only of the corporation's profits. They will switch quickly and effortlessly to another service or product.

Another example. Not too long ago the airline business was in terrible shape. Because of the proliferation of carriers, planes were flying off half empty; there was no coordination among carriers, no way to balance the load of travelers during peak periods, and no information sharing. This was ruthless competition in its purist form. Unfortunately, it was driving everyone to bankruptcy. In fact, in just one decade, the airlines lost more money than they had made collectively since the inception of commercial flight. So, after years of losing money, the airlines got together and did for airline booking what banks did for ATMs. They established a common, shared, open transactional format that allowed all the airlines to see the passenger load, schedules, and even the pricing of all other airlines, even their fiercest competitors. It's called the SABRE system. Crazy as it sounds, airlines decided the best way to avoid bankruptcy was to let all competing airlines look at how many seats were booked on each flight, and even more outrageous, allow competitors to actually book seats on one another's flights, very much the way travel agents function.

Some thought this co-opetition would doom the industry by driving prices down. After all, the "magic of the marketplace" (a.k.a. secretive, ruthless, dog-eat-dog competition) was short-circuited. But what happened was remarkable and surprising. The airline industry has flourished and seen record profits, all because the combined resources of the entire industry focused on serving all the customers' needs. Is it even possible to imagine an airline starting up today that didn't belong to this open-environment SABRE system? In a situation like that, anyone using the SABRE system could book passengers on all but the new airline. That would be analogous to a new bank setting up ATMs that only its customers could use, or a long-distance company that only allows calls to other members of its system, and no one outside of it. It's easy to predict what would happen. No one would go to a non-SABRE airline, because they couldn't participate in the expansive choices offered by SABRE system members. And quite frankly, any start-up airline that didn't join SABRE's co-opetition arrangement would be doing so only in the hopes of monopolizing customers—a futile effort, even for airlines that already have regional markets cornered.

Customers have no interest in being monopolized or treated as if they have no options. The customers have no interest in being the victims of a company trying to limit customer choices so it can make a bigger profit. Customers have shown again and again that they will stick with a company that puts customer service ahead of profits, even if it means sending the customer to a competitor. That's because the customers' only real interests are having their needs met conveniently, economically, and efficiently. When basic levels of service and safety are met, they have little interest in who takes care of their needs, though they will demonstrate fierce loyalty to companies that consistently do so with superior levels of service. Companies that try to corner the market or limit customer choices will only earn customer resentment, because these customers—increasingly savvy and informed, increasingly empowered to switch services and products in an instant—will look around and find out that there were other choices and savings they were denied.

CO-OPETITION AND SERVICE

There will be an increasing number of co-opetition relationships as the interactive marketplace and e-business communication tools come into full bloom. That's because one of the great advantages of Internet-enabled commerce is that it breaks down and frustrates monopolies by allowing consumers to view aspects of transactions that were previously concealed behind the scenes. Today it's hard for a company to convince customers that it is the "exclusive" agent for a product or service offering, when the customer can click his or her mouse and see it for sale elsewhere. (No matter how big a company is, it's going to see an exponential decline in market share if it tries to build walls of exclusivity.) These days it's going to take a lot of talking for a company to convince customers that it has the best price and service, when

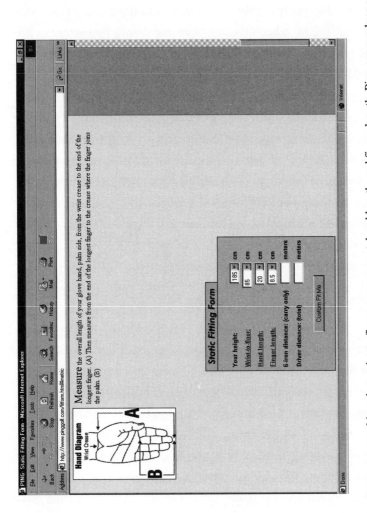

Figure 7–1 When a consumer enters his or her wrist-to-floor measurement, hand length, and finger length, Ping can produce a custom golf club. Other options include shaft type, color, club length, and grip.

they can click a mouse and compare prices and service instantly from a wide variety of vendors who can serve them on an individual basis. To get an idea of how Internet-enabled commerce will rewrite the rules, imagine what the Internet and e-business tools would be doing to the airline ticket booking industry if the SABRE system never existed. The Internet is its own SABRE system. Web sites can instantly compare prices, seating, and flight availability. (In fact, a leading airline-booking Web site, Travelocity.com, is run by SABRE!) If SABRE didn't exist, the Internet would have invented it, piecemeal, through its ability to centralize, cross-compare, and make transparent all the interactions and commerce that in pre-Internet days were closed, secretive, monopolizing, and whose profit was often derived from the fact that customer's access to information was purposely limited. Given current technology, companies that are afraid to offer their price and inventory information for comparison will find enterprising entrepreneurs assembling that information piecemeal from a variety of sources and formatting it for easy customer access. When that happens, those companies that insist on secretive monopolizing will be left with nothing around them but the walls they've built trying to keep customers in. (For examples of this, just look at the world of auto pricing or the pricing for airline tickets.)

Now let's take this one step further. For an ever increasing number of industries, Internet-based e-commerce is doing to them what the SABRE system did for the airline industry: Load-balancing and allowing customers transparent simultaneous views of all competitors' options and prices. These new systems are also allowing consumers to act on their own behalf, where previously agents intervened, only to charge a premium for access to so-called exclusive information. But perhaps the most remarkable thing about co-opetition in a world of Internet-enabled transparent commerce is that the focus of our economy is shifting away from products and shifting onto service. Why? Well, when on the Internet and there is remarkable similarity of prices and designs for similar classes of products, the company that's going to get the business is the one that offers the superior service. The task of searching for the quality product at the right price will now take place on the Internet, often with automatic search engines using product specs and price ranges entered by the customer. (Some prices will be so similar the customer will compare *only* other aspects.) Customers will still wisely shop for products, but they will be looking even harder at the branded service that comes with the delivery of whole-product packages. They will be looking for what's attached to the product to make it more valuable and convenient for them, like customization, personalized warranties, automated follow-up service keyed to their personal calendar, and preferential links and discounted access to allied companies whose services or products they've indicated they may want to consume. So, in a sense, our economy won't be thrown on its head: The same number of products will be consumed in all sectors of our economy and at lower cost to both the consumer and the producer; the same suppliers will deliver them, albeit much more efficiently and cheaply. But there will be a shift in priorities, *from* shotgun appeals and hype led by superstar spokespeople, *to* highly targeted, even individualized, appeals to specific customer; with "knowledge of the one"; *from* erratic prices *to* predictable transparent pricing, *from* mass market *to* mass customization and individualized service. Companies that want to survive will not focus solely on price. Prices will find their own levels. Companies will instead focus on how well they can deliver whole-product services that cater to each consumer's individual needs in a way that retains their loyalty. These are the whole-product services that customers will be willing to pay more for.

CO-OPETITION IN A ONE-TO-ONE WORLD

One of the main consequential benefits of co-opetition is that it will force or at least encourage a single common format for economic exchange. If co-opetition doesn't create a single common format for *all* economic exchange across all industries and all computer platforms (that's the ideal situation), it will at least force it among participants within an industry, as seen in the airline and banking industries. Single common formats force all the players in an industry to open a transparent exchange, as seen, at least in a fledgling form, with airline tickets. But look for this kind of co-opetition transparency to open up other industries that have—in pre-e-business, preinteractive marketplace days—kept their systems closed to everyone except the customers they have tried to monopolize or treat as captives. Imagine the benefit to consumers if, for instance, all plumbing supplies from all the manufacturers were all on the same universal system. It would be fantastic. When a customer needs to fix his Moen washerless ceramic cylinder faucet, he simply goes to any store's Web site and uses a simple code or ordering protocol that was established by a consortium of cooperating manufacturers. When he looks for ceramic cylinders he won't have to worry if the ones he is pricing will fit, because he will know that from the system. And since a number of manufacturers will be offering that part at essentially the same price he will buy the one that comes with ancillary service that makes the part more valuable to him, such as extended warranties, installation tips videos, or discounts on other parts. Not only will this kind of universal system benefit consumers of plumbing supplies, but just think of what it can do to simplify and make transparent the buying and selling of such things as car parts, computer components, anything at all. Gone will be the days where manufacturers set up artificial walls—be they walls of difficult pricing strategies, or proprietary, exclusionary designs and codes—constructed only to contain customers, baffle them into frustration, and force them to buy a similar product they could have found elsewhere for less.

With that in mind, think back to Chapter 3 on one-to-one marketing. Through the use of Internet-enabled computers, increasingly high-speed data transmission, and clever e-business systems, any company's computers will be able to tell customers apart using in-depth customer profiles, no matter how many customers they deal with. These same computers will allow a company to instantly provide one-to-one service to any number of customers as though each customer's needs were the sole focus of the entire company's attention. Finally, through e-business, companies will be able to respond, one-to-one, to a customer's service and product needs by using the customer's individual input to customize the delivery of a service or the custom manufacture of one-of-a-kind products. Now add in the fact that systems serving these customers will be integrated into a procedural-based system that will streamline and make seamless the otherwise cumbersome communication among all parties involved in the production and delivery of any product or service. That will be possible because all the players involved in the delivery of a service or product will be making decisions based on perfect, complete, and current information. That information will be presented and exchanged using universal systems and access, coupled with information willingly surrendered by the consumer and product or service provider. What do you end up with? Well, let's modify an earlier example.

Imagine a world not far from now where the airline industry—not just an individual airline, but the industry at large, a consortium of *all* the carriers—has established a one-to-one relationship with each of their customers through a personalized e-business link to their computers in which they've entered information about their wants and needs. Since the airline industry will be sharing this information through open formats, each and every vendor of airline tickets is aware of each customer's preferences and billing information. But they are also procedurally linked to the customer's personal computer and its calendar. Now, let's put this engine to work. Let's say a woman wants to go on a trip. Instead of calling American Airlines or Delta, wading through their voice mail, and talking to a service agent after a long wait, she simply goes to her computer, calls up a regional, national, or global map, and, using the configuration-management approach discussed earlier in this book, simply drags and drops her points of departure and destination. Then she drags and drops her dates and times. Moments later, her integrated system finds a choice of airline, flights, and prices. She drags and drops her choice into an "Accept" box, and in another moment she gets an e-ticket receipt. She's on her way. Billing is simple too, because the system can easily be tied to her personal or business accounting and banking systems.

What has happened? Well, using the customer profile as the basis for selecting flights, seating, and payment method, all the airlines electronically competed for the woman's business. If a choice of airlines is offered—if a choice was requested—notice that the air tickets are basically the same price. The customer ends up choosing an airline based on which one has historically given her the best service, or which one offers some perks for purchasing their tickets, above and beyond what other airlines are offering that day, e.g., meal or taxi vouchers, discounts at hotels, bonus frequent flier miles, free first-class upgrades based on your "gold status," etc. Further, since there are other services air travelers typically consume, the airline that was chosen can key the delivery of these services to the customer's calendar, based on her departure date. Let's say that her profile, lodged in her Web page, has made it known that she needs to have her luggage repaired and her dry cleaning delivered to her destination location. Since she's indicated she wants these services and she's also indicated what she is willing to pay for them, they can be arranged automatically. All taken care of by the airline that booked her ticket, all procedurally tied to her personal calendar and customized to her specific needs. Will she choose that airline again, given the choice? Absolutely. Do you think she'll even pay a premium next time for one of their tickets, knowing that all these services are a part of the package? You bet.

Now take this example and apply it to the example used earlier of a broken faucet. By calling up an exploded diagram of the faucet on an e-business link to the local distribution centers, the products and parts are offered by a consortium of co-opetition-based plumbing supply houses. They will all be using a universal product system, and prices will necessarily be competitive among consumers of the same volume level, since these prices can be so easily viewed side by side. What will make the products different is the level of service attached to each one. So, using the diagram of parts, the customer drags and drops the desired part to a "Search" box. Instantly, the company that has the best price and fastest delivery of the product appears. If two supply houses come back with the part at the same price—as will be increasingly likely in the transparent world of e-business—then the choice is based on the service or extras offered by the vendors, e.g., free overnight delivery, coupons for other purchases, frequent flier–type points for customer loyalty, or instant messaging to a local prequalified plumber. Indeed, if a truly robust profile is developed with this vending consortium, they might even know that the faucet was still under warranty and offer the part for a steeply reduced fee or free, as they volunteer to submit the warranty claim or send someone to fix it at no cost, billed automatically to the original supplier.

This search-purchase using drag-and-drop configuration management within the one-to-one marketing framework is not so far-fetched. It *won't* take decades, for instance, for industries to realign in the face of explosively more powerful computers and Web access 100 times faster than it is today. And once the technology is available it won't take long before savvy customers determine how to take full (and ruthless!) advantage of it to find savings, reward companies that have been good to them, and punish (by simply shopping elsewhere) companies that have tried to monopolize them.

ONE-TO-ONE VENDORS WILL BENEFIT TOO

Remarkably, the benefits of this economic revolution aren't limited just to consumers. They also pass along benefits to the businessperson at the distributor and manufacturer level. After all, this world of the interactive marketplace isn't all about just the consumer saving oodles of money and reaping the benefits of high-quality service and limitless choices. It's also about astute, forward-looking companies making oodles of money by cashing

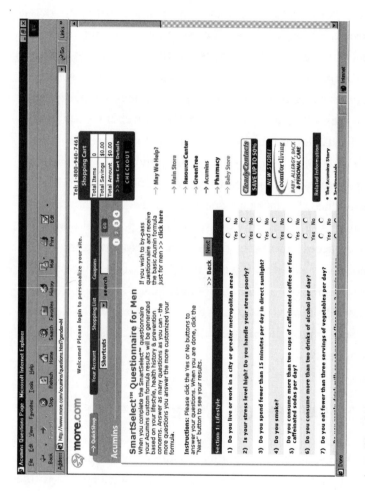

Figure 7-2 By answering a lifestyle questionnaire on More.com's site, consumers can actually custom-create vitamins to suit their individual requirements and symptoms.

in on the dynamic opportunities offered by e-business. Let's take a close look.

Let's take a construction company in a small city. A man runs this business with the full knowledge that there are a dozen other construction companies out there that do essentially what he does, at essentially the same cost. To put even more pressure on his company, he knows that these dozen or so companies, combined, can easily produce far more houses in this city than could possibly be consumed, even if interest rates dipped to 4 percent and down payments were allowed at 2 percent of the house's gross cost. Clearly it's a buyer's market—as it often is in so many industries these days. How will customers be picking and choosing the construction companies? Well, after they assure themselves of a basic level of quality construction (knocking out, say, half the available companies) they will base their decision on service. The construction company that will get the job is the one that can provide superior, personalized service, for the best price, on a one-to-one basis (as robust as the examples of one-to-one service offered elsewhere in this book).

As these construction companies realize this, they will all start to compete fiercely for this limited business. Sound familiar? Actually, it sounds frighteningly like the way airlines used to compete, as they drove each other into bankruptcy. So, let's apply the same co-opetition relationship among fiercely competing builders to see if it can load-balance the industry in their local area, and make everyone profitable. This arrangement would first demand that all the competing companies share the same open format for all their transactions, kind of like the SABRE system. They can share the same software package, or use an e-business platform that allows cross-platform transactions. Ideally, they will all use the same integrated, procedural-based project management systems or those that can talk to one another. Next, they need to be willing to let their competitors share their job information, and be able to easily borrow and contribute resources, if it serves the purpose of profitably serving customers' needs. Third, this new co-opetition consortium has to recognize that not every department of every company within the consortium will be guaranteed survival. This isn't necessarily a bad thing. It's not necessarily "downsizing," because the co-opetition relationship may force some interesting discoveries. For example, these construction companies may find that one company's salesperson actually works best as a liaison to the various suppliers. He or she can best be used not for sales, but as an agent who seeks out consortium alliances. In another realignment, a worker or two freed up from accounting duties by the redundancy-defeating features of integrated software can now find the time to set up Web pages for each of the jobs underway, or integrate links for even more efficiency to the back offices of all the supply houses serving their jobs.

What's more, these efficiencies aren't related just to office personnel. What competing framing crews from a number of different companies in pre-co-opetition days may find is that, when ganged together as one large crew, they can frame houses far more efficiently. That surely would be more profitable than a scenario where smaller crews start and stop occasionally for projects and then sit (expensively!) idle until another job comes along.

Other economies can be found by combining research efforts that can bring all the participating companies savings. Six separate design-and-bid teams, working for six different highly competitive builders may not have had time for the research on the best services and products at the best prices. But now with a co-opetition arrangement, research duties for these design-and-bid teams can be split up and delegated: One team in one company can work on researching and purchasing doors for everyone at good prices with iron-clad service guarantees, another team in another company can focus on windows, another on lumber, another on roofing.

No matter what the various arrangements are that get produced by these co-opetition relationships, as long as they are focused on profitably serving the customers' needs and enhancing the house-buying experience for the customer, they will make the co-opetition relationship stronger.

Is it impossible to believe that competing companies could cooperate in this way? Is it impossible to get this many people to agree on a common software and format, or to share resources in a world as competitive as the building industry? Well, the test that proves the rule, the building industry, now is a concrete example of how this can work. A case study of just such a co-opetition consortium of builders in Manassas, Virginia, showed how successful the co-opetition arrangement can be. This group of 44 builders works together, load-balances the available work, buys land and materials together, shares subcontractors, labor, and materials—on a daily basis. This arrangement has proved amazingly profitable, far greater than the businesses would have shown had they worked alone, struggling mightily, reduplicating efforts, to try to put their competitors out of business. As a combined unit, they can each serve their customers better.

It is important to note that these "competitors" do not work in secret. They openly embrace their co-opetition alliance. In fact, they broadcast and advertise their relationship and brand their superior, low-cost service as a group. They present their synergistic arrangement—and the savings and superior service they assure it can pass along—as an asset over other construction companies that are trying to move into the area. And just like customers who won't open accounts at banks that have a limited number of proprietary ATMs, or customers who won't use non-SABRE airlines, potential home buyers have repeatedly chosen the branded, low-cost, service-oriented co-opetition construction consortium over the services of the large single, lone-wolf construction company that can't offer the robust one-to-one service and savings. As a result, the consortium just gets stronger and stronger. That strength is rooted, as it should be, in serving customers first. That's what makes this co-opetition consortium a success in this brave new world where the business community is increasingly seeing death to competition as it knows it. If this kind of customer-focused open system is alarming, just consider the two industries who have applied these processes and profited because of it: airlines and banking. They are now more profitable than ever, even with the leveling out of prices for their services.

THE DEATH OF COMPETITION AS WE KNOW IT?

Co-opetition doesn't mean that companies will strop competing. There will be natural competition among companies within a co-opetitive alliance and from companies outside of a co-opetitive alliance. That healthy combativeness will remain. But it is clear that the Internet economy will shake out those companies that are not interactively linked or that use technology to monopolize the customer. As a result, these old-fashioned companies will be left to wither and die, as they see their customer base dwindle. So, the death of competition as we know it for those companies will be one of customers lost to a new way of doing business. Where will the customers go? To the interactively linked companies that are competing against one another on a whole new level, using the transparent economic system, supercharged by the Internet, to their competitive advantage. But just like Daimler-Chrysler, IBM-Lotus, AOL-Netscape, and IBM-EDS-Oracle-and-Sun, these companies see a profitable future through alliance building, not wall building.

8

C H A P T E R

The Vortex Effect

EXECUTIVE SUMMARY

As companies involved in co-opetition share resources and move toward using common-format, open-platform, transparent systems for pricing, supply chain management, and access to products and the means of producing them, all the players in these e-business consortiums will begin to engage in alliance building that benefits anyone who participates in any aspect of the interactive marketplace—manufacturers, suppliers, and customers alike. This is especially true when that commerce is undertaken on a one-to-one basis that's integrally, seamlessly linked to the consumer. Indeed, as these unique alliances gain members and power, they will take on a "vortex effect" that draws more and more economic activity in by the very nature of the alliances' efficiencies and approach to business. These vortex alliances will consequently create a reciprocal disadvantage to companies that try to set out from scratch to build their own private interactive systems or that use closed or proprietary formats in an attempt to monopolize an industry, a segment of an industry, or even a product category. As a result, the companies engaged in co-opetition will be able to create unfathomable opportunities to reduce costs and further open standards, which will inevitably invite even more customer control, as the vortex alliance system becomes a "trusted intermediary" whose shared resources will work with untold efficiency to supply notoriously reliable, timely, just-in-time services and products, and an ever increasing ability to command and manage the supply chain for cost efficiency.

The ultimate purpose and mission of any vortex alliance is to serve the customers' existing needs and desires and predict their future needs and wants. Given the capabilities offered by the e-business co-opetition-based vortex systems proposed in this book, all of that will become evident, accompanied by the return of high levels of customer satisfaction that have drifted so far from with mass-market commerce. Customer satisfaction and service will again take center stage and be the driving force behind the survival or extinction of any alliance or its members.

Who benefits from the vortex effect? Everyone who joins in the system of open commerce and symbiotic alliances: manufacturers, buyers, sellers, suppliers, and most of all, consumers, who will truly appreciate—at last!—the control they have over their choices, buying decisions, ability to customize products, and access to a transparent pricing system. These consumers will demonstrate their appreciation for the sellers' respect of them by being fiercely loyal repeat customers. After all, what would be the incentive for them to go anywhere else? They will naturally use more services and systems offered by companies in this trusted intermediary alliance vortex, which will then grow to offer more services that attract more satisfied customers, all of which will create an economic community that's beneficial to all who participate and welcoming to all outsiders who see the benefit of customer control.

About 25 years ago, a revolutionary new gas engine hit the market. It was called the Wenkle engine, and it was unique because it was based on the efficiency offered by centrifugal force and the laws of thermodynamics, namely that a body in motion tends to stay in motion through its own inertia. When the Wenkle engine started, it wasn't very efficient. It had to get going first. But as it gained speed, unlike a piston engine, it actually got more efficient the faster it went. The more momentum the internal parts of the engine got, the less energy it took to keep the engine going, until it seemed to take on a momentum all its own, requiring very little energy input to keep it up to speed.

Remember that group of 44 builders discussed in Chapter 7, the case study on co-opetition? These were the builders who—though fierce competitors—agreed to use a common-format system and work together to load-balance the available work, share resources, and buy as a unified group. What made this arrangement unique was that, like the Wenkle engine, it wasn't very efficient when it started out. There were adjustments in corporate culture to make, business systems and processes to standardize, and communication systems to tie to all the various players. Plus, tasks had to be reassigned as emerging efficiencies moved and realigned people, shifting their talents from jobs with broad, often all-inclusive responsibilities to jobs with specific focus. But as this system gained momentum, as it gained speed and everyone became well-versed in how everyone else's business ran, it gained a momentum all its own. It gained an efficiency that increased in quantum leaps for every quantum leap in commerce flowing through the co-opetition system. And once it got up to speed, it required less energy input to keep going. In fact, it only got more efficient with use, as every dollar spent within the system on goods and services saved the dollars that—in pre-co-opetition days—were spent on redundancy, reduplication of information (both among competing companies, and even within a company's own various subsystems), costly material, and advertising and marketing sales campaigns that weren't able to effectively capture the market.

Keep in mind that what inspired this co-opetition consortium to exist at all, and what drove and focused it to perfect itself as a profitable entity, was the singular mission of providing the highest customer service at the best price. In fact this model group of 44 co-opetition builders can now charge a premium for their houses because of the consumer-service benefits offered by their alliance. (Think back to the example of four grocery stores, where after prices level out and services were added, each store could charge *more* when competing than if it were the only store in town.) This group of builders is not an isolated case. And it won't take but a minute of research to find that this arrangement is now springing up all over the nation. Look at Daimler-Chrysler, IBM-Lotus, AOL and Netscape, and IBM-EDS-Oracle-and-Sun mentioned in Chapter 7. These are companies that realize the advantages of establishing alliances with their competitors, yet—and this can't be stressed enough—they are not doing it to form monopolies, but instead to open the markets, reveal their ideas to one another, and establish formats that are not meant to exclude vendors and allied businesses, but to welcome them.

What's also important to remember for anyone wondering how to survive in the world of e-business is that the astute forward-looking businesses engaged in this new form of commerce have been careful to note three crucial things. First, for the vast majority of industries, there has been more than enough manufacturing and service-delivery power to provide more than ample supplies of products and services to the world. Second, customers in the age of e-business are able to exercise their choices of which products to buy with unprecedented ease (low switching costs), as they click their mouse, or instigate an automated search through the transparent interactive marketplace for the best quality-service combination (remember, prices will have leveled out among similar classes of items). And third, since there are so many choices among industries with fierce competition, and customers are exercising their discretionary power readily and with increasing ease, any company that will survive must be centered on a selfless customer-service mission. Now let's see how these principles work in practice.

THE VORTEX EFFECT

A central premise of this book is that companies or consortiums of companies that will flourish in the e-business world of the interactive marketplace are the ones who reinvent themselves not as businesses trying to corral customers, but as companies that welcome competition. These companies join forces selectively with their competitors, because it will be the only way to keep the customers coming back. This joining up of companies will be best enabled by computer-to-computer exchanges of information, either across platforms using transactional code-to-code mapping programs, or through systems that can directly communicate with one another using automated information exchange. As companies join forces and make alliances, reaching out to form one-to-one enabled affiliations with the widest possible range of companies of any possible benefit to their customers (even reaching out to companies that have no apparent relationship to the service or product they produce), they will find—as the 44 builders found—that their co-opetition consortium will gain an unstoppable momentum in at least two ways. First, if the companies in the co-opetition consortium enact the self-perfecting "learning loop" one-to-one relationship made possible by e-business, the efficiency of that consortium can only grow, as it takes advantage of all the members' combined resources, customer information and profiles, data sharing, automated sharing of time-sensitive information about customer needs, efficiencies generated by common platforms, and the seamless secure transfers of financial information and funds. But more importantly, the co-opetition consortium will not only grow as a result, it will see a powerful vortex effect, that, counter-intuitively, has a natural tendency to gain momentum the bigger it gets. How? Because of the co-opetition consortium's power to provide such a wide range of personalized, thorough, unique services at near-commodity-level prices, it will see an exponential increase in the number of customers drawn in because of that service and pricing. This is called the vortex effect because, like a whirlpool vortex, it will get stronger as more energy is fed into it, and because it takes on a force and momentum all its own, becoming a self-feeding system. The ever increasing number of customers are drawn in to take advantage of an ever increasing number of companies supplying goods and services with ever increasing efficiency and with ever more carefully refined customization of the products specific to the customers' needs. Indeed, by taking advantage of shared customer profiles, and computer-to-computer links to them, companies that are part of a vortex will be able to predict the specific, singular needs of individual customers they haven't yet done business with and haven't even met, an *unprecedented* feat in the history of commerce.

Even better, the vortex effect generated by co-opetition companies will be so strong that it will frustrate startups from "going it alone" (e.g., closed-system ATMs, non-SABRE airlines, unaffiliated builders). But though the vortex will seem to create a monopoly all its own—something that will actually frustrate customer service—it won't be a traditional *exclusionary* monopoly, like when someone tries to corner the market (Rockefeller with oil; the Hunt brothers with silver; AT&T with long-distance phone service). Instead, it will be a natural monopoly which, when centered solely on profitably serving the customer's needs, will welcome anyone who can add to the efficiency or make the service package more robust, more of a whole product, in a boundary-free transparent system of transactions that rolls forth. For example, a customer-driven juggernaut of free choice, free markets, and ever increasing efficiency. So, in effect, bear witness to a revolutionary reversal of traditional economic patterns: The vortex will be a natural nonexclusionary monopoly created not by the manufacturer or service vendor, but by customers through their patronage. Think of it as a customer-created monopoly.

Now let's apply some nth-degree thinking here. Imagine an economic system (regional, national, worldwide) in which the vortex has proved so beneficial to both customers and businesses that everyone in the economy has joined it, a co-opetition vortex where everyone—consumer and provider alike—uses one single format, seamlessly sharing information, taking advantage of alliances to find efficiencies, and tying all economic exchange integrally to consumers' lives. This is a system that consumers will welcome because of the savings and convenience it offers and the ability consumers will have to choose and switch away from vendors who aren't responsive to their slightest whim (remember "complete customer control"?). What will happen as a result of this isn't very difficult to predict. Apply nth-degree thinking, play out the logical extension of this, and it becomes obvious that the Internet and the e-business it enables—continuing a trend strongly, unstoppably underway now—will drive prices to common levels among similar classes of products. And with prices so similar among similar categories of products, how will consumers make choices? What will they use to decide which service to buy? Well, let's answer that by looking at how companies will naturally respond to a leveling of prices. The successful company will not just sell their products and services, but be helpful in selling others' products too. As long as it benefits the consumer, it will pay for any vendor to seamlessly, transparently bring to consumers the customized, just-in-time products and services delivered by *any* of the companies linked to them through e-business, whether or not those products and services are directly related to them or not. In a scenario like this, a company that sells organic skin cream could easily share, through e-business links and alliances, customer profiles that enable its customers to find a quality roofer, a vacation bungalow in Mexico, or a rare collectible first edition of an Ernest Hemingway novel. How? Each player in the vortex becomes part of the trusted intermediary's group, whose word—or links and alliances to other trusted intermediaries—is as good as gold when recommending and predicting the services a customer will want or need.

Far fetched? Not at all. Web-based commerce—the most rudimentary form of e-business, and just the beginning of what will be available in just a few years—is making momentous strides toward this now. There is only more dramatic change coming as business-to-business e-business companies start linking computers to one another and enabling the automated exchange of information. But keep in mind, the Internet works best when it enhances existing products and services. The vortex effect is nothing new in economics, it is simply a phenomenon made dramatically, infinitely more efficient by the Internet's ability to accelerate and enable co-opetition-based vortex consortiums.

As a brief example just to reinforce this premise and make it more convincing, let's look at a contemporary example: gaso-

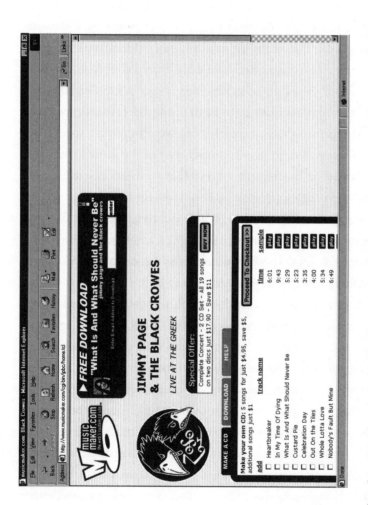

Figure 8–1 At Musicmakers.com, there is a selection of songs that you can choose from to create a custom music CD. Click, add, and print, and your own custom CD is on the way to you.

line prices. The price of gas from gas station to gas station is pretty much uniform. Since the economy has driven the gas price to an even level (it may go up and down, but does so uniformly for all vendors), people don't really look at prices, or if they do, they recognize that, though it may be high, it doesn't change much from vendor to vendor. So, how does a person choose where to buy the gas? He or she chooses the station that offers the most helpful ancillary services at the best prices, like convenience shopping, a team of good mechanics, an assortment of good food, frequent user credits, free car wash, pay at the pump, etc. Once price is out of the picture—something e-business will bring about—the various stations will compete on the basis of service and the whole product. Now, which approach is more likely to succeed, the station offering the whole product or the going-solo, standalone, stripped-down provider who just has a low-cost pump and nothing more? The answer is clear.

As this dynamic plays itself out, the gas station can create its own vortex by becoming an economic community center, where people gather not just to buy gas but to visit, get coffee, get reliable directions or references for, say, landscaping services, house painters, or a good bakery (or even become a bakery providing jelly donuts if the need is there). As the gas station becomes a trusted intermediary for information and referrals, and becomes more of a whole-product vendor, more and more people will come there to do their business. Any gas stations nearby that try to compete solely on the basis of price or that serve only gas will either go out of business, or increase their service to create their own whole-product offering, and simply join the vortex.

The difference that e-business brings to this example of competing gas stations is that the Internet can establish alliances without being limited by geographical or categorical boundaries. What's more, these alliances can be created in seamless integrated ways that share information with their customers on a one-to-one basis. Note that the leveling of pricing won't be limited to just gas, but to nearly every product or service that people consume. By adding value to these products and making them part of whole-product offerings, prices will naturally rise again, but the value will be measured in an entirely new way. Value will be a function of the comparison of one value-added whole product to another, even though the consumer knows they can get the commodity version of this product elsewhere for less. Let's take the example of Hertz rental cars briefly discussed in Chapter 6. Through attentive customer service, value-added loyalty programs, and alliance building with hotels and airlines, Hertz has managed to turn a hefty profit even though they charge above-average rental car prices in a tight commodity-price-driven market. Because of this positioning, Hertz is already ahead in the e-business game, and others will have to follow. As more companies follow Hertz's lead, Hertz will have to stay on its toes because consumers are already finding they can switch rental car companies with great ease, just by clicking a mouse. Consumers are already making these decisions using early-adopter Web sites that allow instant comparisons among rental car companies, and billing that is integrated into trip planning, air ticket purchase, and hotel reservations. With these examples of where the economy and e-business are going, every businessperson should ask himself or herself if their company is ready to provide products and services to customers who have this kind of discretion. Better to be prepared, because these are the new rules for every kind of company, not just rental cars, airlines, builders, and banks.

THE TRUSTED INTERMEDIARY

Customers will naturally be drawn to such a co-opetition vortex. After all, it has been demonstrated again and again that customers always look out for themselves. If they misperceive—that the co-opetition consortium were only focused on trying to corner their markets, limit their choices, or draw them in with one low-cost service only to keep them captive by dictating who they should buy all their other services from, then customers will shy away. Customers as a rule always look out for their best interests, as they should. But what's remarkable is that the co-opetition consortium always will be looking out for their best interests too. It will do this on an individual, one-to-one basis, as it standardizes language among players (more on this in a minute), enables customization of products, provides just-in-time delivery, and keys product and service offerings to customers' individual personalized calendars, all features of the interactive marketplace discussed throughout this book. When a customer uses a co-opetition consortium's service for something they need only occasionally—say an auto tune up, or the services of a house painter—they will be able to readily compare service and prices. Indeed, well-positioned companies will be encouraging them to compare service and prices. And when they use the service as repeat customers, it is because they have found the service consistently satisfactory. (The provider who delivers subpar service won't be able to remain part of the consortium for long, as a kind of e-business "natural selection" will weed out bad companies on an ongoing basis.)

Let's look now at typical consumers' behavior when they get what they pay for from an attentive vendor. The consumers develop a level of trust in that vendor. Since it's human nature to ask for referrals, even for unrelated products and services, it's typical for people to ask the supplier of one high-quality service for a recommendation of another, perhaps wholly unrelated, category of product or service. Isn't that how it has always worked? Someone who does a good job in one area generally knows the companies that do good jobs in other areas. A good mechanic—a stickler for making sure all the right parts are in the right places—probably knows a good cabinet maker; a good cabinet maker may know a good doctor; that doctor knows a good pharmacist; that pharmacist knows a good banker, who knows a good investment counselor, and so on. Well, the provider members of a co-opetition-based e-business consortium, a vortex of companies who participate in open-format information- and resource-sharing arrangements, will engage in very much the same "neighborly" referral system—very much like what is seen in village-based economies discussed in Chapter 1. But now, with e-business, the service and product providers will be engaging in this referral system in a highly sophisticated, integrated, seamless way that is dramatically advantageous to both the vortex alliance members and the customer. This system tracks the transaction, integrates essential information where needed, and follows up by rewarding all involved who helped make it work. The co-opetition-based e-business consortium becomes a *trusted intermediary*, where consumers can comfortably engage in commerce with *any* member company (whether they've done business with them in the past or not), because the mere fact of the company's presence in the consortium assures all involved of a basic level of service and quality.

OPEN PLATFORMS

One practical matter alluded to elsewhere in this book, yet not fully explained, is the trusted intermediary's role in establishing transaction standards. There are a number of terms to describe this, such as "open platform," "open transactional format," and "common format." What these terms all refer to is a form of digital language and coding that all the members of the vortex or co-opetition alliance agree to speak when they engage in transactions, and it's absolutely crucial to have this in order to get optimum efficiency out of the system. If the various members of the consortium don't speak a common language, then it's imperative that they use a common e-business platform that enables transactions across platforms. To highlight the importance of this, just imagine how frightfully inefficient and expensive it would be for even a small number of co-opetition alliance vendors to do business together if they didn't have a common language and common product and job coding. (Unfortunately, this is the situation among many vendors today, *preintegration*, and why as things change there will be the 35 percent supply-chain savings discussed in Chapter 6.) The confusion generated by vendors who do not share common systems, for even simple nonintegrated transactions already costs a fortune. Imagine how it would skyrocket when vendors start combining their products and services integrally with other vendors. The cost of translating information from one system to the next, and rehandling and reentering information along the way would be staggering. If this is surely the case among a small number of vendors, imagine how complicated this translation and coordination of formats would be among the computer systems of 1000, 10,000 or 100,000 different integrally linked vendors serving a vast array of data (a completely possible scenario as these vortexes grow). Just think of the coordination that would have to go on so that a whole product involving six vendors and a dozen products were offered and billed to one customer. Imagine what mighty corporate accounting systems would be tested to the breaking point trying to supply, ship, track, and bill for their products as they were commingled with a number of other company's products, *if* they did not speak the same language. It would be like a room full of people all trying to do the same thing but who all spoke different languages and used different currencies.

So, one of the challenges of the trusted intermediary is to establish *and diligently maintain* a commonly shared computer exchange standard that allows the seamless exchange among all the vortex members of product information, pricing, e-cash transfers, etc. There will be a natural tendency for companies that want to dominate the vortex to establish their own coding system. But that's a play for unnatural domination of the alliance, and the cost to the consumer will only be limited service or partial (instead of whole) products. One company would gain an advantage not on the basis of the merit and natural selection of its product or service, but on the basis of its ability to monopolize information and corner customers, something contrary to the co-opetition system and the natural order. In fact, once a so-called trusted intermediary starts taking sides, the natural order of the customer-centered-focus is diminished, and another vortex will be created to enable a purer economy with complete customer control (remember the ATM example in Chapter 7).

Let's end with another practical question: Since so many vendors won't want to undertake the costly task of rewriting their product and transaction codes to a new standard, but still want to participate in the vortex-based co-opetition alliance, what steps can they take, and where does that leave the customer? Well, the true trusted intermediary, the trusted intermediary that is really focused on customer service will do that translation for both the customer and the vendor. It would be as though someone came into a store speaking French to a shopkeeper who spoke only

German and a supplier was in the back room that spoke only English. The trusted intermediary wouldn't require them to all learn a new common language. Instead the trusted intermediary will learn all of their languages and translate back to all the parties involved. Only, in the world of e-business, it won't be languages that the trusted intermediary translates, but product codes. And the translation will be the seamless integration of those product codes across differing platforms and formats so it looks to the customer—large or small—as though the vortex members all speak the same language. The customers can come to the trusted intermediary knowing that when they buy a whole-product package that includes products from six different vendors, like Grohe faucets and American Standard sinks, they won't have to buy these things piecemeal at five different locations using five different manufacturer's codes, and five different billing systems. Instead, they will find that—with all pieces guaranteed to fit together perfectly—they can come to one shopping, shipping, and billing source and let the trusted intermediary figure out the transactional details from there. A single source serving multiple needs. And isn't that what customers are after? One-stop shopping where they can mix and match among product types, confident they will work together. Billing will be a single seamless transaction as well, not five or six payments to five or six suppliers, even though five or six may be serving you. Easy one-source shipping—even of custom preassembled products—will be enabled in this way too.

Just think of how closely focused the economic exchange will be in this common-format, co-opetition-based system, how precisely targeted the selling and delivery of products will be, and how quickly bad service providers or poor-quality products can be weeded out and exiled from the referral program. (Think of how expensive, by comparison, a multistandard system would be.) Think of the opportunity the customers have to express their wishes individually through their profiles and how those profiles can be integrated into the product manufacture and delivery systems of all the players involved. Think of the economy and savings such a system will create, and think too of the loyalty and trust this system will engender in the customer. Customers will enter into e-business relationships to purchase something they are familiar with, confident they won't get duped or taken advantage of, because the system has a natural incentive to provide them with a good experience. And when these same customers go to purchase something they are *unfamiliar* with and need advice on—like a new furnace, mutual funds, medicine, floral arrangements, new cars, driveway paving—the co-opetition consortium will again and again prove itself to be a "trusted intermediary"—the arbiter, the advocate, the thorough researcher, the price evaluator, the ever vigilant protector. Each and every customer will be able to trust that the companies allied in the co-opetition consortium will act in their supreme best interest every time. And this will only add to the vortex, as the customer returns again and again for all manner of services and products, knowing that the allied companies will prove themselves to be the customer's advocate. The system can only grow and get stronger, and it will do so based on the trust (and ever increasing efficiency) generated over and over again with each transaction. Finally, the system will only get better at serving the various customers' needs, because each of their profiles only gets more refined with use, so companies can more precisely predict what products and services they need and when.

WHEN COMPUTERS RULE THE WORLD

This book proposes a world in which computer networks know and share vital, personal information about customers, including their credit, preferences, and profiles. This information is shared among companies that are trying to make money selling things to you. And some of these companies never will be contacted directly by the customer; they will be suggesting products and services based on buying patterns or implicitly expressed desires. It seems like a formula for a world spinning out of control, where everyone with a product or service that *might* be appealing to the customer will be using communication channels to contact that customer in the hopes that they will only be used by a few. This is similar to what today's telephone has become (and the reason many people rarely give out their unlisted cell phone numbers). Another valid question is whether a world like this will truly make a marked improvement in people's lives, because it can easily be construed that in a future 40, 50, or 60 years from now computers will have sorted out the "haves" and the "have nots," and though computers will be everywhere, people will be living pretty much at the same economic level that they are living at now. Is it possible that computers will only accelerate the speed of different transactions, and not improve the lives of the people who are using them?

When states sell drivers' license information to marketers and then charge to remove a name from the list, that is abuse. When credit card companies distribute incomes and buying patterns by zip code so that a person's mailbox is stuffed with strange catalogs, that is abuse. When telemarketers phone at dinnertime, offering unwanted products or services, that is abuse. When a catalog company that a person has never contacted before calls and is able to provide that person's name, address, and credit card company, that is abuse. But the e-business strategy presented in this book is not a system that is open to that kind of abuse. Indeed, it's designed to stop it.

How? Computers offer the ability to exert supreme, precise control over the information contained in them or networked by them. And it should also be clear that an interactive marketplace offers supreme trackability, where transactions can be graphically followed with ease every step of the way, including easy access to who broke the rules by sharing transaction information without an individual's permission. But this e-business system is one that exists on the basis of privacy and tight control of information (soon to be enacted by privacy laws that will demand it). When an individual enters into an economic exchange using the current pre-e-business system, by using a credit card, the person ultimately loses control of that information. It becomes the de facto property of the vendor, as unfair as that seems. Worse, no one can track the information. If the Mobil credit card company or Visa decides to sell a name to AAA car services or a book club, the individual doesn't have much say in the matter. Furthermore, AAA or the book club probably couldn't even disclose the card company that gave the name away in the first place. But in a one-to-one interactive e-business exchange the customer will be the sole person exercising complete control over what information is shared among product and service providers. Even better, the customer will know the value of his or her name, and when it is profitably shared within the system, he or she will share in those profits, either directly or through discounts at allied companies. He or she will be able to release information on a need-to-know basis, and he or she will be given the power to withdraw from the system with the click of the mouse. The customer will also be able to punish by exclusion and exile any entity that abuses his or her information or uses it to cause him or her any distress or inconvenience. Think of it as a super sophisticated "call blocking," and it is the kind of security offered by the trusted intermediaries. They will not abuse your right of privacy or control access, because the abusers will be ruthlessly replaced, as the customer demands back the control. This is the interactive marketplace.

This is a future where efficiencies create sustained economic booms and a steady rise in individual wealth. A future where the customer is in absolute control. Let's step forward into the interactive marketplace and take our places in that future now.

9

C H A P T E R

Community Is the End Game

EXECUTIVE SUMMARY

This book is not about technology. Though it puts forth business plans that depend on technology; business plans whose features and functionality are embedded in technology, this book is not about how to use technology to create a business. Instead, it is about community; about how community-building is the most essential aspect of a successful technology-enabled business plan. Why? When a business is dependent on technology (a Web page, a browser, a unique graphic interface, a piece of software) that business plan is only as unique as the latest version of the technology, only as good as your last marketing campaign. Switching costs to other systems are extremely low for users who are simply hunting for the next best functionality. Moreover, the latest technology and the cleverest marketing plan are things your competitors can (and will) buy to put others out of business.

Instead, this book is about the success that will come to companies that focus first on community building, as they enable that community with the latest technology. Why? When a business

231

has an installed user base of customers who use a common technology (or various technologies that can be data mapped to one another), that business can leverage that user base to bring a variety of for-sale products and services to it. The B2B parent company that is unifying these platforms in not like an old-fashioned, product-line focused company that sends out an army of salespeople to sell stock items to customers. Instead, that company and its sales force become agents that bring a variety of products and services to the community, as the parent company concurrently upgrades and enables that community's technology. (Look at how AOL is now giving its software and service away for free in Britain and for low cost in the United States. AOL is *not* selling technology; it is gathering community and bringing for-sale products and services to it.) True B2B community-based companies are not Web-dependent business plans; indeed, Web pages are madly proliferating, infinitely dividing the attention of Internet users. Nor are true B2B companies static "click-and-buy" services. The successful business plans imagined herein are *pure* B2B plays; business plans that entwine satisfied users in their systems and protocols; business plans that have "stickiness."

Yet the community-based businesses that keep users coming back are not doing so by trapping the consumers, but because consumers are drawn and attracted to return to the B2B system for its range of products and services and the commanding consumer control these systems allow (these are the traits that unify all the companies cited in this book: Cisco, Dell, Nike, Ford, GM, Lands' End, Ping, etc.). Moreover, this stickiness also exists for the supply chain side of these systems, as provider companies are drawn into the systems' protocols so they can gain access to the community the parent business has assembled. The product manufacturers and suppliers will find it continually profitable to link their ERP systems to others in a system that allows data generated at any point in the supply chain to seamlessly migrate to and populate the back-office systems of any other linked (even dissimilar) system. Yet their contact with their consumers isn't based on technology, but on *relationships* embedded in the profiling data and in the cross-platform data migration abilities that allow multiple vendors to exchange data effortlessly. These are the technological features that allow personalized one-to-one service which the customer would have to build from scratch, purchase-by-purchase in another system, or perhaps go entirely without at a click-and-buy Web site. The ability to expand and maintain these relationships is accelerated and amplified by technology, but the relationships themselves are not dependent solely on technology. They are not quite so portable nor so shallow. If they were, the company that invented the next best technology could steal these customers away, and the customers would have reason to demonstrate allegiance... not the case in a true B2B system.

Once community-based, cross-platform data sharing has been enabled, and configuration-management tools are in the hands of the customer, it is a small step to linking consumer needs to critical-path–managed systems that can predict needs and allow the supply chain to load-balance its inventory to respond on a just-in-time, or even with custom-direct, basis. Currently, the supply chain fills these needs wastefully, on a just-in-case basis, with a shotgun approach that floats out stock products that just might get purchased. It's a system that guesses at need. So the residual benefits of this B2B community-based business plan are multidimensional. Besides the costs saved by automating the information flow among component systems (perhaps 4 to 8 percent of the product cost for each link in the supply chain) it is completely possible to foresee 20 to 35 percent net savings for

the delivery of custom products direct, a capability made possible not solely by technology, but by a community enabled with
technology.

A true B2B system is often a product-neutral, business-prac-
tice-neutral system whose cross-platform data transmission capabilities allow participating companies to innovate by absolving
them of the irksome task of data mapping to dissimilar platforms,
and by establishing a master, universal SKU hierarchy at the parent B2B hub that allows unencumbered, free, fair, true B2B commerce to take place. Based on these principles, and balanced on
this B2B backbone, companies that have consumer-facing B2C
applications are free, alas, to truly innovate: A manufacturer who
has had the capacity to make and deliver custom products, but
who has lacked a cross-platform-enabling tool or a way to collect
field data, can now deliver those custom products direct at 20
percent less cost. A supplier who spends 6.5 percent of its gross
costs *reshipping* unsold stock products in the field because they
weren't consumed as the consumption models projected can now
target stock deliveries, or even deliver just custom products. Using the systemwide transparency of a true B2B system, a manufacturer can now buy raw material based on real, not projected,
need. Consumers, long contained by the availability of limited
varieties of stock products, can now take control of the design,
cost, manufacture, and delivery of unique products that are only
limited by their budgets, imaginations, and the rules of physics.

Community-based B2B systems allow users to respond
rather than react; predict rather than guess; specify rather than
ask. They are clearly the wave of the future, the way all business-
to-business and business-to-consumer sales will occur; they are
the business model that ever improving technology will most ca-
pably serve. To do business otherwise, using paper-based mod-

els, or with enterprise resource planning (ERP) systems that can't communicate across platforms to allied systems, would irreparably hinder a company's ability to profit, especially when up against constantly improving B2B systems that become vortexes that draw more and more community members in and that get increasingly efficient with use. Why not take profitable advantage of this new economy? Adapt and apply the principles in this book. Be a part of, not a witness to, the most dynamic revolution to sweep through the business world in 150 years.

Index

Acumin (company), 97
Advertising, 18–19, 137–138
Alliance building, 214. *See also*
   Co-opetition
Amazon.com, 1, 9, 43, 62, 163
   future of, 167
   one-to-one marketing and, 78–79
   vs. Barnes and Noble, 183–187
American Airlines, 16–17
America Online (AOL), 59
Apple Computers, 138–139
Automobile industry, 46–48

Banana Republic, 39
Barnes and Noble, 9, 163
   future of, 167–168
   vs. Amazon.com, 183–187
B2B model. *See* Business-to-
   business (B2B) model
B2B2C model. *See* Business-to-
   business-to-consumer
   (B2B2C) model
B2C model. *See* Business-to-
   consumer (B2C) model
Ben and Jerry's Ice Cream, 153
Brandenburger, Adam M., 189
Branding, 132, 136–137
   future of, 143–149
   interactive, 149–155
Broad Vision, 68
Browser-based model of retailing,
   1–3
Business-to-business (B2B) model
   community-based, 232–235
   defined, 3–6
   transactions in, 40

Business-to-business-to-consumer
   (B2B2C) model
   integrated cross-platform of, 9
   interactive, 6–13
      features of, 7–8
      keys to successful, 10–11
      savings and, 10
Business-to-consumer (B2C) model,
   2
   browser-based, 9
   switching costs in, 9–10
Buy.com, 9, 43–44, 168

CDuctive, 96
Chase Manhattan Bank, 192
Cisco Systems, 60, 61–62, 122, 174,
   232
Citibank, 191–192
Commodities
   customization of, 117
   e-business and, 132
   transparent economy and,
      136–143
Community, 45
   building, 231–235
Companies. *See* Vendors, one-to-one
Competition, future of, 190–191,
   208–209
Computers, 27, 228–230
Configuration management. *See also*
   Mass customization
   customization and, 54–62
   defined, 56–57
   future of, 59–61
   process of, 58–59
   smart, 117–124

Consumers
    changing habits of, 62–64
    configuration management and,
        the 54–61
    controlling, 38–45
    distinguishing apart, 74–78
    mass customization and, 125–126
    product creation and, 7–8
Cooperative arrangements. *See*
    Co-opetition
Co-opetition, 189–190
    airlines example of, 193–194
    ATM example of, 191–193
    benefits of, 199–203
    building industry and, 205–208
    service and, 195–199
Critical-path management, 103
Customers. *See* Consumers
Customer tracking, 33–35
Customization. *See also* Mass
    customization
    for commodities, 117
    configuration management and,
        54–62
    one-to-one, 96–98
    vs. proceduralization, 46–48

Dell Computer, 10, 42, 60, 61–62,
    110–111, 125–126, 138–139,
    232
Disintermediation plays, 186–187

Ebay.com, 9
E-business. *See also* Interactive
    marketplace
    advertising and, 137–138
    business-to-business sales, 62
    house-building and, 81–84
    interactivity and, 79–80
    one-to-one service and, 80–81
    successful companies, 165–167
    survival and, 214–215
    switching costs and, 132
E-commerce, defined, 79–80
Electronic digital messaging, 129–130

E-loan.com, 9
E-mail, 92
    interactive marketplace and,
        128–130
Enterprise resource planning (ERP),
    2, 16
Exxon, 27

Fashion industry, 136–137
Ford Motor Company, 27, 59, 108,
    232

Gap, 39, 187
Gateway, 125–126, 138–139
General Motors, 59, 232
Grand Union, 77

Hertz rental cars, 164, 221
House building industry, 48–50
    co-opetition and, 205–208
    one-to-one marketing, 81–87
    tracking system for, 179–182

I2 (company), 68, 78
Industrial Revolution, 24–27
Information Revolution, 27–28, 29–30
Information sharing, 11, 228–230
Instant interaction, one-to-one
    marketing and, 88–92
Integrated systems, 4
Interactive B2B2C model. *See*
    Business-to-business-to-
    consumer (B2B2C) model,
    interactive
InterActive Custom Clothes, 96–97
Interactive marketplace, 20–21,
    31–33, 127–128
    assembling, 169–173
    efficiencies in, 157–161
    e-mail and, 128–130
    integrating, 175–179
    mass customization and, 129–130
    *n*th degree feature of, 133–134
    tracking transactions and, 229
    transparent, 136–137

Interactivity, 33
    instant, 88–95
    results of, 70–71
    rewriting rules for, 65–66
Intermediaries, trusted, 222–223
    challenges for, 225–227
    transaction standards and,
        223–225
Internet, 6
    economic exchange and, 15
    retail sales on, 17
    sales on, 17
Isuzu, 176

J. Crew, 146–148
JC Penney's, 39

Lands' End, 62, 113–116, 232
LL Bean, 39, 187

Mass customization, 96, 104–106,
        124–125, 132–133. *See also*
        Configuration management;
        Customization
    consumers and, 125–126
    history of, 126–130
    interactive marketplace and,
        129–130
    mass production and, 106–117
Mass production, 106–117
Match Logic, 78
McDonald's Corporation, 51–53
Microsoft, 27, 28
More.com, 204
Musicmakers.com, 219

Nalebuff, Barry J., 189
Name brands, 136–137
Nike, 108–109, 139–141, 232

One-to-one customization, 96–98
One-to-one marketing
    co-opetition and, 199–203
    defined, 72–74
    examples of, 78–81

One-to-one marketing *(cont.)*:
    house building and, 81–87
    instant interaction and, 88–92
    winning with, 98–101
One-to-one service, e-business and,
        80–81
Open platforms, 223–227
Oracle, 59, 108
Owens Corning, 151

Peapod.com, 187
Peppers, Don, 71
Ping, 196, 232
Pontiac-GMC, 113
Proceduralization
    McDonald's and, 51–52
    vs. customization, 46–48
Product codes, 226
Product creation, consumers and, 7–8
Retailing
    future of, 21–20
    Web-based, 1–3
Rogers, Martha 71

SABRE system, 135–136, 193–194,
        197
Service, co-opetition and, 195–199
Shopping cart model, 79–80
Stickiness, 9–10
Supply chains, 5, 9
    enhancing, 174–175
    Wal-Mart, 182
Switching costs, 9–10, 44
    e-business and, 132

Technology, 1, 8, 65, 171, 231
Toolsonline.com, 187
Tracking systems, 33–35, 180–181
Transactions
    in B2B model, 40
    tracking, 229
    trusted intermediaries and,
        223–225
Transparency, 8, 136–138
Travelocity.com, 197

Trusted intermediaries, 222–223
    challenges for, 225–227
    transaction standards and,
        223–225

Vendors, one-to-one, 203–208
Vortex effect, 211–212, 215–217
    gasoline prices example, 218–220

Wal-Mart, 5–6, 39, 41–42
    supply chains of, 182–183
Web-based retailing, 1–3
Winn Dixie, 77